KALI
—Linux—
HACKING

A Complete Step by Step Guide to Learn the Fundamentals of Cyber Security, Hacking, and Penetration Testing.

Includes Valuable Basic Networking Concepts.

ETHEM MINING

First Published in the United States of America in 2021

Copyright © 2019 by Ethem Mining

ISBN: 978-1672429733

ABOUT THE AUTHOR

My name is Ethem Mining, I was born in Baltimore in November 1973. It may be a coincidence, but it's the year the first computer was installed in the White House. Technology has always been something fascinating to me, almost like a magnet. I wrote my first program when I was just 13, a banal program written in PASCAL, but it was mine. I could use my imagination.

During my studies I got closer and closer to the world of cybersecurity, a wonderful world that puts your knowledge to the test all the time. You always must be one step ahead of those on the "dark side", who are people exactly like you, passionate about information technology and with great skills. It is an incentive to stay up to date.

For some years I have wanted to transfer my passion to others as well, so I decided to write a series of books dedicated mainly to beginners, to introduce the wonderful world of Linux, programming and cybersecurity.

I leave you my email contact, don't hesitate to write me for suggestions, requests and, first of all, criticism. Every single email I receive will be a source of growth for me and I will give importance to each of them.

Thank you and have fun reading

ABOUT THE PUBLISHING HOUSE

EVEROOKS LTD WAS founded in 2019 as a small independent publishing house. The idea of the name comes from the fusion of two words, "forever" and "books", to show our love for books.

Our favorite quote is by Marcus Tullius Cicero:

> *"A room without books is like a body without a soul"*

Today we have grown considerably, to become one of the most interesting realities on the market, managing to support various authors in their projects. We publish fictional and non-fictional books, audiobooks and ebooks on all major categories and genres.

Our mission is to guarantee our readers quality books, books that can answer your questions or that can entertain you during your moments of relaxation.

Our team consists of

- 4 writers
- 2 reviewers
- 1 translator

We want you to know that you too can contribute to our growth, and help us to improve the quality of our services more and more. In fact, by leaving a review (especially on Amazon) you will allow us to submit our book to more and more readers, thus helping us to be able to expand and help many other authors.

For this I would like to say **THANK YOU** right now!

Please feel free to contact us for any questions or information on **everooksltd@gmail.com**

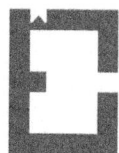

Everooks
Your Books...Wherever You Want

Table of Contents

INTRODUCTION

Have you ever been in a situation where you wanted to try hacking something? Maybe you wanted to test the security of something that you were developing or you simply wanted to challenge yourself, and you were unsure of where to start. If this is something you have considered, Kali Linux may be the OS you need to begin the process.

It is important to note that Kali Linux is not for everyone—you need some level of familiarity with how Linux works or at least an idea of how to interact with Linux if you wish to use Kali Linux in a useful manner. If you do not have this familiarity, it may be in your best interest to go back and begin the study of a simpler distribution of Linux, such as Ubuntu or Mint before beginning to tinker with Kali Linux. If you do decide to move forward with Kali Linux, keep in mind that the tools within this distribution can cause serious damage if misused, and could potentially even lead to significant consequences. This is not a distribution to be taken lightly.

If you decide to proceed, this book will give you the beginner's guide to Kali Linux and how to use it to begin hacking.

The first half of the book is dedicated to giving you the basic knowledge that will be needed to truly get the most of the You will be given information about hacking and how it has made cybersecurity more important than ever. You will learn the basics of networking itself, diving into several different concepts and how they work. You will learn all about Kali Linux—what it is, how it is installed, and how to use it, and you will learn several of the most basic Linux commands.

In the second half of this book, you will begin to discuss the utilization of Kali Linux for several different purposes. You will learn about Nmap and how it can be used to detect and exploit vulnerabilities.

You will be guided through the steps of remaining anonymous. You will dive into Metasploit and how to make use of it with Kali Linux. You will learn about digital certificates and how to use them, and finally, you will learn about bash (Bourne Again SHell) and Python scripting and why the two of them are sometimes considered to be at odds despite the fact that they could very well work together and cooperate to get much better results than if they continue to be left separately.

By the time you have finished reading this book, you will have an idea of the foundational information you will need to first decide whether Kali Linux is for you, and if it is, you will know how to get started with it and have an understanding of just how powerful this distribution of Linux is. While Kali Linux is not for everyone, if you do happen to fall into the category of people that would find use in this program, then the tools that will be provided with this distribution are incredibly valuable assets that you will not want to miss out on having in your arsenal.

At the end of the day, you will be able to determine if you are happy with the idea of Kali Linux and whether this is for you or if instead, you should be making it a point to move on to a different distribution of Linux instead. You will be able to decide if you want to continue to work entirely with the shell or if you want to learn Python instead. And, if none of this that has been discussed makes any sense, then by reaching the end of the book, you should find some clarity with the topics at hand and how they should be used.

PART ONE

Introduction to Kali Linux and Hacking

CHAPTER 1
What is Linux?

It is one of the worst things that could happen to many people—they log into their bank account or credit card only to realize that their account balance is completely drained or that someone has been making heavy use of their credit card. This can absolutely devastate many people, and unfortunately, these days, this is a very real concern.

These days, financial information is backed up somewhere. Your bank has a record of your account number, your card numbers, and everything else someone would need to access it. You likely log in somewhere to pay credit card or utility bills.

You may even do the bulk of your shopping, both for groceries and other times online. This means that your personal information is constantly being used online. You enter your social security number to apply for a credit card. The three major credit bureaus keep your information, tracking and regularly updating it. You may even apply for taxes online.

This has one serious implication—all of your essential information is available online somewhere.

To be fair, this information is usually stored behind all sorts of safety protocols that are put into place. They are meant to protect your information from being leaked to people who may be interested in using your information for nefarious purposes, but just like armor, there is usually some way to get through it.

Some systems may be safer than others but at the end of the day, a dedicated individual would be able to find some way to break through if they put in the effort.

As soon as they break through that security system, they have access to any and all of that data, which can then be released and sold, ultimately leading to you having your identity stolen.

Everyone wants to avoid that unfortunate outcome, but with the storage of valuable information comes the risk of attack and exploitation, which must be accounted for.

What is Hacking?

Hacking, then, is the act of identifying any sort of weaknesses within a computer or network's security system and then exploiting that weakness in order to gain the necessary access to whatever is hidden behind the firewall.

For example, a common example is the usage of an algorithm designed to identify a password in order to sort of digitally pick the lock of a network or account. That account has then been exploited to get the desired access.

Hacking may not always be done with the intention to harm— some people do so for legitimate means, such as to locate a flaw in the system to repair it. Others may choose to do so in order to entertain themselves, not unlike doing a complicated puzzle or trying to solve increasingly complicated math problems to test and hone abilities. Others still do so in order to steal information for some purpose, whether to use it for financial gain or to cripple the system that they are hacking. Hacking can come in several forms, such as tricking someone into clicking on an attachment in an email that will grant access to a computer.

Other forms, however, require far more technical knowhow, developing the ability to trick and trigger the system to grant access and information that should otherwise be safeguarded. This book will primarily discuss methods related to technical expertise rather than using backhanded attempts to fool someone into granting access in the first place.

Essentially, hacking is the act of getting into someone else's system, but the methods of hacking can vary greatly. Each of these occurs in different manners and serve different purposes, but the end result is the same—they allow for information to be stolen and used, or for programs to be used in ways that they were unintended to be. For example, some people may hack their video game console to run emulators to allow them to play ROMs of different games, including some that may not have been intended to be used on that system in the first place. Others may use their skills to steal information and sell it to people looking to steal an identity.

Nevertheless, there are numerous options for a hacker to use in order to gain access to all of the information they desire. The rest of this section will discuss some of the most common hacking methods that are out there, allowing you to get a glimpse into what hacking can entail. Keep in mind that this list is not exhaustive.

Malware

Malware is malicious software—shortened down into one word. It includes software such as viruses that are installed, either by you clicking on something that allows it to be downloaded or downloading it yourself, but once you allow it in, you have compromised your information. Attackers will generally use a link or an email attachment that appears to be harmless in order to trick you into installing whatever malware was hidden within.

The installed malware can cause all sorts of issues, such as monitoring the usage of the computer, such as keystrokes, which then allows the hacker access to all sorts of information that may be personal or sensitive. It can also grant full access to the computer, depending on the malware that was installed. Overall, however, the vast majority of the time, the user of the computer will have to do something that triggers the download of the malware.

Session Hijacking

As will be discussed later, when a user is browsing the internet, the user's computer sends several transactions to the website's servers, allowing the website to see who is accessing it, what is being requested, and sending the proper information back to the user to display. This is done via routers and networking, and when done properly, you are able to access the information requested without issue, whether you are simply browsing through sites and clicking on links or whether you are entering in sensitive information.

This data is supposed to stay private, given a specific session ID that allows the server to know who is using it and how it is able to send the specifically requested data back to the individual asking for it. However, sometimes, that data gets intercepted.

Essentially, what happens is that someone else is able to access that unique ID. They are able to use that same ID and make requests as you during your interaction, allowing the attacker to see any of the sensitive information. Sometimes, instead of just observing and intercepting information, the attacker can act as either the website or as the individual using the website, allowing the attacker to request and intercept information from either direction. When this happens, it is known as a man in the middle attack.

SQL Injection

SQL (usually pronounced "sequel") is an acronym for the structured query language. It is the programming language that is primarily used as a means of communication with databases.

When a website or a company needs to store sensitive and critical information, such as patient or financial information, the server that it is stored in will most commonly utilize SQL to manage it.

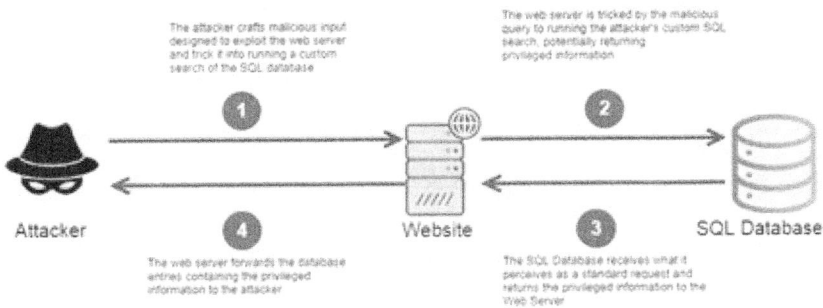

The attacker crafts malicious input designed to exploit the web server and trick it into running a custom search of the SQL database

The web server is tricked by the malicious query to running the attacker's custom SQL search, potentially returning privileged information

1

2

Attacker

4

Website

3

SQL Database

The web server forwards the database entries containing the privileged information to the attacker

The SQL Database receives what it perceives as a standard request and returns the privileged information to the Web Server

The SQL injection, then, seeks to use code designed to trigger the server to provide information that is normally protected. Especially when the server is holding important personal information, it can be a valuable target—that information can either be sold off or used as leverage to blackmail.

Effectively, the SQL injection attack exploits one of the known SQL vulnerabilities, which the attacker takes advantage of. This could be done by inserting a specific code into a search bar or otherwise engaging with it in a way that triggers unintended results.

Phishing

For those who know better than to open up a random attachment or link that has been sent to them, there are other methods to use to trigger you to click. The attacker may know that you are not likely to simply open up a random attachment, so they make the reason to open said attachment one that is compelling and motivating. These people will often imitate other people in order to make you click on the link.

For example, you may receive an email from someone claiming to work for the IRS and saying that you have an outstanding balance with them. They do not specify the balance, but they include a statement attached to the email that you are required to click to see it. Of course, the entire situation is fake. There is no balance owed, and if you were smart, you would remember all of the warnings that go out every year about how the IRS will only contact you via snail mail.

Phishers rely on you not knowing what you are doing, getting too curious, or not being cautious enough to go through the process of double-checking sources before downloading a document.

DOS

Have you ever tried to leave a big event from a small town? Especially if there is only one road that accommodates leaving, you may get stuck in traffic for hours.

The same kind of occurrence can happen with websites—usually, the servers are only able to accommodate so much traffic, and if traffic gets too bad, the website is overloaded and cannot load the necessary sites for anyone. Sometimes this happens legitimately, such as if highly desired tickets go on sale at a specific time that is anticipated to sell out, or during massive, limited quantity sales.

However, sometimes, an individual may decide that they want to see that sort of full stop happen. When they do so, they intentionally flood the website with traffic—so much that the site's servers can no longer accommodate the load, and no one is able to access anything. Known as DOS (Denial of Service), this attack usually comes from a single source all at once.

However, sometimes, it comes from several IP addresses at the same time, using different computers to attack and making it harder to track and stop. This is known as a DDOS—Distributed Denial of Service

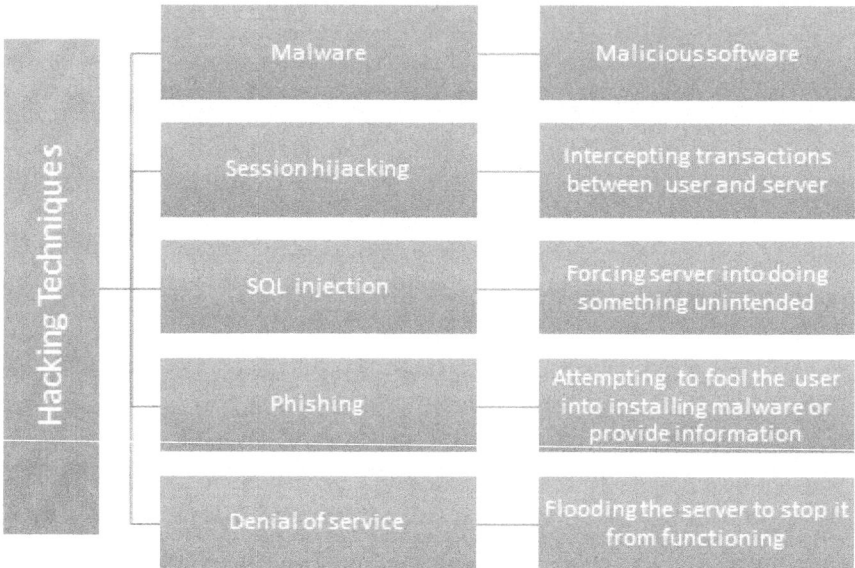

Hacking Techniques		
	Malware	Malicious software
	Session hijacking	Intercepting transactions between user and server
	SQL injection	Forcing server into doing something unintended
	Phishing	Attempting to fool the user into installing malware or provide information
	Denial of service	Flooding the server to stop it from functioning

Reasons for Hacking?

Ultimately, the reasons for hacking can vary greatly from person to person. Some people do it to learn more information. Others do it to cause harm. Others still do it for entertainment or just to learn how. It has become trendy in modern pop culture to discuss the hacker as a major threat to the internet and cybersecurity. This can make for a particularly convincing villain in a story or film, but real hackers are just as capable of wreaking havoc. On the other hand, there have been politically or socially motivated hackers who use hacking to get attention toward a specific event or to bring forth sensitive information—these people are known as hacktivists.

No matter the reason for hacking, one thing is for sure—unless the hacking is done in order to help prepare the system that is being hacked in order to better the security, hacking is dangerous. It is harmful. It is not a toy. It is not something to be taken lightly. If you are in this book because you want to hack someone or exact your own revenge on someone because of something that has happened or you simply want to watch the world burn, stop. Close this book.

Go find a hobby doing something that is not going to potentially ruin lives. Ultimately, lives have been ruined by hackers before. Hackers have been able to destroy people, their livelihoods, their careers, and sometimes even their families. Through the stealing of identity or funds, or through causing a disruption so large that a company has gone over or with any other negative implications, hacking can hurt people, and it should not be treated lightly. This is exactly why cybersecurity is such a rapidly growing field.

Typically, people will have one of four reasons to maliciously hack a server or computer:

- They seek to gain financially, such as through stealing credit card numbers

- They build up their reputation within the hacker community through hacking and leaving some sort of identifiable mark on it

- They are engaging in corporate espionage—the attempt to get a hold of a competitor's sensitive information to get the upper hand in the marketplace

- They are entering a government-sponsored hacking attempt to get national intelligence, weaken infrastructure, or just to wreak havoc.

These people do not care about the rules or laws, and in fact, have created a need for cybersecurity and cybersecurity laws, which will be discussed later within this chapter. People hacking into databases and servers has led to a need to make sure that these are more secure than ever, leading to the creation of the entire field of cybersecurity jobs. Hackers are usually classified with titles referring to hat colors. They may be black or with, red or green, or even blue. Understanding these hat colors can help you get a better grasp on why people may choose to hack, more specifically than the four reasons listed above. It may also help you clarify why you have a desire to learn to hack via Kali Linux yourself.

Black Hats

When you think of a hacker, it is most likely a black hat—they do so for nefarious reasons. These are the ones who are often found breaching servers and exploiting weaknesses. They do so to steal and make money. These people, though criminal, are also making use of some of the most basic techniques that are learned. Though they are quite intelligent, they are motivated by less-than-honorable means—all they care about is what they stand to gain.

Grey Hats

Grey hat hackers are a little more complicated than black hats. They are hacking to steal, but usually on less nefarious terms. They may be interested in sharing files or breaking into software in order to use it without paying licensing fees.

They are usually interacting with servers and networks in ways that are exploitative, but not necessarily to steal the information within it. Instead, they treat their hacking more like a hobby that they enjoy.

They typically will not inform sites when they have found exploits, but they are likely to offer to fix it for a fee. Essentially, these people are more motivated by seeing themselves and proving to others that they are important.

Red Hats

If we were discussing the personality alignment chart right now, red hats would be the equivalent of the chaotic good player— they are interested in stopping black hat hackers, but they do not want to feel like they are constrained by rules and laws. Instead, they will intentionally subvert any authority and go about their attempts by their own rules. If using the expression fighting fire with fire, the red hats will fight a torch with a flamethrower— they aggressively attempt to destroy the black hat's access to the networks upon figuring out who the black hat is, with the intent to render the black hat completely incapable of doing any more harm.

Though these people tend to exist further out from the rest of the hacking community, they tend to be some of the most sophisticated, wanting to play by their own rules.

Green Hats

In the hacking community, green hats tare the beginners. They are usually attempting to learn how to hack in the first place, and will readily ask for help or seek out new knowledge. They are motivated by their desire to learn and develop their skills, ambitiously following their dreams without necessarily having any clear path that they want to follow. However, because they lack life experience and technical knowledge, they also stand to be some of the most dangerous because they have not yet learned just how dangerous their actions can be, nor do they know enough to reverse any damage that they have done.

Blue Hats

Blue hats care about revenge. Though they can be malicious, normally, they only channel their attempts to hack toward whomever they feel has wronged them. Usually, they are relatively new to hacking in general, possibly even script kiddies, but when something bad happens, they may decide to put their newfound skills to good use and set out to intentionally and maliciously hack a target. They do not want to better their skills—they only want to have the technical skills to cause problems.

Script Kiddies

These people do not get a color, but they are still important to mention. These people are usually uninterested in stealing information, but they still find enjoyment in taking codes that are already created and injecting them into servers in an attempt to cause problems. They are most likely to utilize their skills in techniques such as a DDoS to flood a website just to annoy people without any real purpose.

Hacktivists

As briefly touched upon, hacktivists are those motivated by politics. They may be lumped into the black hats, though they are usually hacking in an attempt to bring to light something of importance toward their cause. They may try to release information or records that are supposed to be kept under wraps, or they may decide to actually cause issues for a company.

They may even attempt to fight terrorist groups thanks to their impressive working knowledge. They are trying to lead to positive change, even though they may be using negative methods to achieve it. They are motivated by their cause above all.

White Hat (Ethical Hacking)

The last classification of hackers is the white hat—these are known as ethical hackers. The ethical white hat hackers typically are hacking in an attempt to bolster defenses. These people are intentionally trying to hack into the software in order to help a company strengthen its own defenses as exploits and vulnerabilities are identified.

These people are most often found in cybersecurity careers, trying to help keep your sensitive information safe and secure from other people's attempts to steal it. These people are often trained in IT security or computer science and then certified by the EC-Council. This means that they must complete an intensive class and pass an exam, which often involves the training on how to handle the most common and current security domains with hundreds of attack techniques and technologies. The white hat hacker must also maintain these credentials with annual education credits.

Typically, if you want to become a white hat hacker, you are interested in helping people. You want to defend people and you want to do it in a way that is lawful, acceptable, and beneficial to everyone involved.

You want to eliminate the vulnerabilities within the system to protect it from damage rather than attempting to go vigilante justice on someone such as the red hat hackers, who may have their hearts in the right place but go about things in a way that is just as bad and destructive as the black hat hackers.

What is Cybersecurity?

As touched upon earlier, the invention of servers and the birth of hackers also brought with it the creation of cybersecurity. Cybersecurity is crucial for those who are intending to rely on servers and databases—without cybersecurity, there would be no defense system. Cybersecurity allows for the defense of any internet-connected system, meaning it protects your hardware, software, and data from falling victim to cyberattacks.

Hackers		
White hat	Motivated by a desire to protect
Black hat	Motivated by greed and selfishness
Grey hat	Motivated by proving themselves
Green hat	Motivated by ambition and learning
Red hat	Motivated by defeating black hats their own way
Blue hat	Motivated by revenge
Script kiddies	Motivated by boredom
Hacktivist	Motivated by politics and their cause

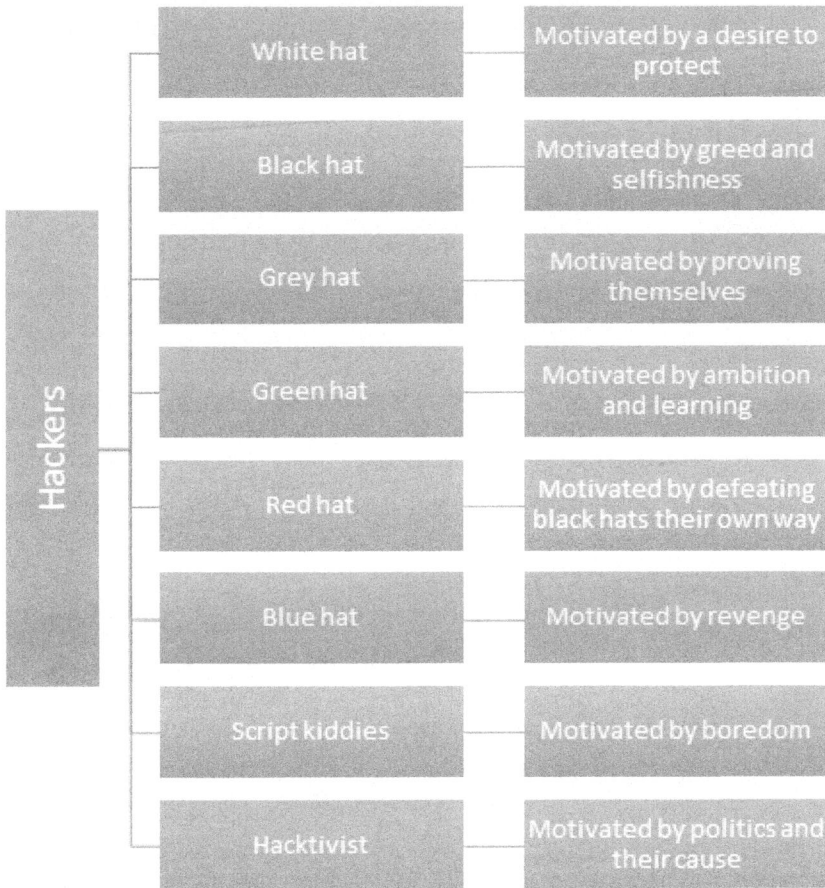

When what needs to be protected is on a server or a database of any sort, there are two different ways that it must be protected—physically from being damaged or taken away, and also digitally in order to protect from those who attempt to access it via the network and steal or harm protected information. Cybersecurity, then, has one specific goal: protecting IT assets from being attacked in order to ensure that the information and data that is housed within those IT assets remain protected and secure for the benefit of everyone.

Because so much data out there is so quite sensitive and should be protected, cybersecurity is absolutely essential. Not only the individual user's data is protected when implementing cybersecurity practices, but the company implementing the practices is also protecting itself. Because the likelihood of a massive breach drops with the usage of cybersecurity, the likelihood of major negative press attention also goes down. Cybersecurity helps lessen the risk of breaches, ransomware attacks, and identity theft of individuals, and though cybersecurity can be difficult to maintain due to the ever-changing world of technology and IT, maintaining it has serious benefits.

Cybersecurity practices should be used by anyone who is using anything connected to the internet—whether you are an employee, an owner of a server, or an individual user, there are steps that you can take to avoid falling for the traps of hackers or those who seek to exploit your data. It all begins with your password. However, there are also many other points where the security of your personal data as a user is no longer in your own hands and it is up to the company in charge of your data to protect it.

Unfortunately, cybersecurity runs into one specific problem that is not likely to go away any time soon: Because technology is constantly evolving and changing, and because networks and data standards change as well, as do hackers, who inevitably find more exploits, cybersecurity is an endless job. There will always be another exploit to find and patch up. There will always be another attempt to steal data. This means that the cybersecurity profession is not likely to go anywhere any time soon.

Typically, these threats are approached by focusing the bulk of the resources on protecting the most crucial components to protect against any threats that are known to be out there and significant. However, this approach also leaves some systems either less defended or undefended or leaving the system open to threats that may be deemed to be less known, or those that are less dangerous.

The Elements of Cybersecurity

Cybersecurity, despite the constant fluctuation and change in the system, also has a series of elements that must be maintained. These elements are essentially the backbone for cybersecurity—it needs to have each of these to be deemed successful and truly protect the data and infrastructure it was tasked with. These elements include:

- **Application security**: This lessens the likelihood that any sort of unauthorized code will be able to find a vulnerability

- **Business continuity planning**: This helps maintain or resume any critical functions if something catastrophic happens

- **End-user education:** Teaches the employees or users how to act in order to protect the information

- **Information security:** Protects information

- **Network security:** Identifies, prevents, and reacts to any threats with security policies, tools, and IT.

- **Operational security:** Classifies information and protects it

Information Security: The CIA Triad

As noted just prior, one of the elements of cybersecurity is information security. This particular element is so important that it warrants discussing in its own section. Within information security, there is a concept known as the CIA triad. This particular triad stands for confidentiality, integrity, and availability, which serve as the mission statement of sorts for the information security side of cybersecurity.

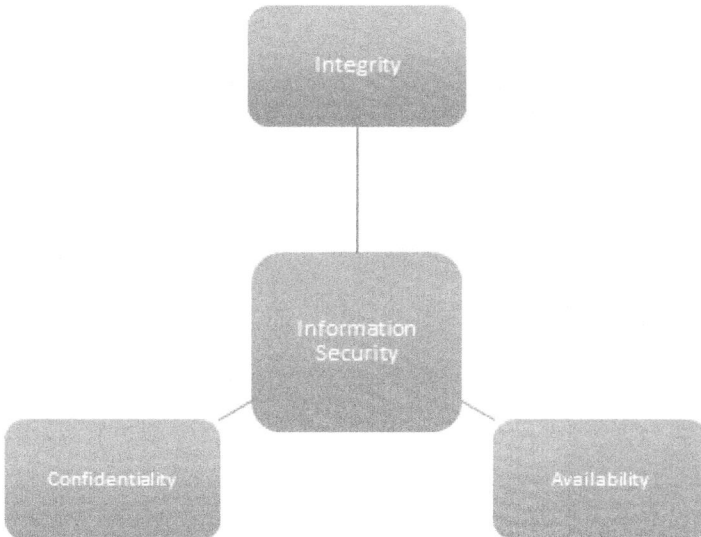

Each of these three sides to the triad is crucial: Information protected must be confidential, accessible, and maintained with integrity. Without achieving all three of these goals, information security has not entirely been achieved. These are the fundamentals for information security, and will always be the core objective.

Confidentiality

This is the ability to protect information from any sort of unauthorized access to it. When information is confidential, it is not accessible by anyone that is unauthorized. For example, when you go to the doctor's office, your medical history is confidential unless you sign a release form. In the medical setting, that information is protected by both security measures as well as regulations for conduct to protect your sensitive medical information from becoming well-known. In the information security side, the information that is being protected will only be accessible by authorized users, with unauthorized users automatically being rejected upon failing to provide the right credentials. For example, consider a credit bureau that has access to all of your personal information, from your social security number to the accounts and account numbers of any of your credit lines—if their data is not secure, you are at risk of identity theft.

Integrity

Integrity is achieved when information is held in a way that is accurate and consistent. This means that its intended and original structures are maintained without any prior authorized changes to the material in the first place. While it is possible that information gets changed if the user is careless or used or if there is an error, however, integrity will be maintained so long as the information is unmodified during storage, being transferred to the requester, and when being used, short of anyone actively and consciously changing it. This means that the data is accurate and kept constant. For example, imagine that you have checked your bank account before going to buy a new computer because you wanted to make sure that your direct deposit check had, in fact, been deposited. If your banking app does not update properly or reflect the fact that you did, in fact, get paid, you are going to think that you are unable to buy that laptop or any other need you may have had.

Availability

The final goal, availability, refer to the information being readily available whenever and wherever it is requested and needed. Because information is generally protected, it is not available to everyone, but it must be available to those with the proper credentials. This should be maintained as much as possible— data protection without ready access to it is not exactly the most useful in situations where data becomes essential. For example, imagine that your medical records are being protected. If your doctor were unable to access your medical records on-demand, you would not be able to get the proper treatment.

CHAPTER 2
Introduction to Networking

With the wide-scale use of the internet comes the introduction of networking. While it may be easy to think that the information or requests that you put through the internet simply appear instantly after being beamed up to a satellite, especially if you are using a router for a wireless home connection, what actually happens is that the data that you push through goes through wires to get the information you have requested to be returned to you, all at lightning-quick speeds.

This is the creation of the network, and whether you have ever considered it or not, it is a massive part of everything in this day and age, and you most likely use the network several times a day. Whether you check your bank account or even buy something with a debit or credit card, you are sending information through a network.

What is a Network?

Defined simply, a network is two or more computers that are connected together in some way in order to share information or interact in some way. The computers do not have to be connected via wire—they can be connected through infrared beams, through the transmission of radio waves or satellites, or even through wires. However, they are always connected in some sort of way.

There are several instances in which a network is a right choice for the usage that is planned out. For example, imagine that you have two computers (a laptop and a desktop), a tablet, and a cell phone. You regularly use all four items at home and want to make sure that data that is attached to your laptop, which you use primarily for being able to access and browse the internet or answer emails, is also available on your more powerful desktop, which may be reserved for more intensive programs, such as playing video games or editing large files or videos. You also, just for convenience, would like to make sure that your photos that you take on the go with your phone are accessible from your other sources as well. When you want that level of connectivity, where you are able to access all of your files from anywhere, you are looking for a network connection. In getting that network connection, you are able to share those files with ease. Of course, there are other ways that networks become crucial as well. If you work for a school, for example, you may be familiar with computer labs.

In these labs, students put in their login information from any computer to pull up the same account. Teachers can also submit their information to log on from any computer on that network as well, so long as they use the right password and username.

Some of the versions of Linux, known as Linux distributions, or more commonly shortened to "Linux distros," will be easy enough to hop right in to using, while others could be your worst nightmare immediately upon installing it, such as Gentoo, which requires all programs, including the kernel, to be built from source. This chapter will guide you through understanding what a Linux distribution is, how to decide which distribution will be right for you and your usage, and then provide you with a brief overview of ten of the most common distributions you can find.

Types of Network?

Networks themselves can come in several different forms. These networks are used for everything and anything that involves the transmission of information, whether you are printing a document or sending an email. It is important to understand that, when discussing networks, you are primarily discussing one of two different network types, though there are several others, depending on the purpose. The two that are most commonly discussed are LAN and WAN, with VPN being a close third. These three types of networks have their own specific usage scenarios. This section will give you a brief overview of LAN, WAN, and VPN, though you will find that VPN gets discussed in more depth in later chapters.

WAN

Standing for a wide area network, WAN allows for computers to connect from further distances apart. This means that computers, even far from each other, are able to be connected to each other through one means or another. This can be on a smaller scale, such as an internet service provider that is connected to several different LANs, stringing them together into one cohesive network together. Another more well-known type of WAN is the internet. The internet allows for the connection of computers across the world.

VPN

VPN stands for a virtual private network. It is a network that has been extended across the internet as if they were accessing a private network that others cannot access, though the internet.

These can also be achieved remotely, through the use of a virtual point-to-point connection, in which the private and remote sites are able to access each other. They are routed through the internet from a private network in order to transfer sensitive information and ensure that it is secure. Typically, it was done by encrypting the data—making it so it cannot be read easily by someone who is not supposed to have access to it in the first place.

Network Address

A network address is a way that the nodes and hosts within a network are able to be identified. Just as your house has an address that allows for snail mail to be delivered exactly to your address, wherever it is, your computer has its own sort of address. By addressing something to your specific address, someone even on the opposite side of the world will be able to send you something. The network works much like that—it allows you to send something to a very specific point, even if you are not connected physically in any way at all.

In fact, you can even send it across the ocean from one continent to another with ease, so long as you are able to send the request to the right place.

In order to really begin to understand network addresses and how they are relevant to hacking, Kali Linux, and understanding computing in general, you must first understand some important concepts. This section will guide you through understanding and defining nodes, hosts, IP addresses, both public and private.

Nodes

Nodes are the individual redistribution point within a network's connection— if you were sending something via snail mail, the nodes would be all of the individual post offices through which the mail passes. If you send something from Alabama to a remote town in Alaska, that one letter is not going to directly travel to that remote town—it is going to pass through several checkpoints that act as redistribution points. The node may also refer to the final endpoint as well. It is effectively every location to which the data has been forwarded until eventually it reaches the end of the line and is delivered to where it was supposed to be.

Hosts

The host is a computer that is connected to another computer that is responsible for sending data. The host is a network node—it receives and sends information and has its own address.

This can be a server that is holding information as an archive, allowing other people to access it. It could also be a person to person host, in which you have one computer that is holding all of the information in which you are going to access from another. In the sense that a host of a party is the one providing the fun, food, and festivity, the computer host is providing all of the information that is desired. In order to be deemed a host, the computer or server must have its own network address.

IP Address

IP addresses are your "Internet Protocol" addresses. This is the unique address assigned to your computer's online activity. Continuing upon the post office model of the network, think of your IP address as the return address in the corner of the envelope—it allows for the network and the website or server that you are accessing to know that it is your particular computer accessing it, and allowing the server to send the proper information as requested back to you.

Without this address being nicely provided for you, the information that you have requested is not as likely to make its way back to you, despite needing to.

These IP addresses are not static based on the computer; rather, they are provided by the internet service provider (ISP) for you. Since the ISP acts as your gateway from your LAN to the internet, it also tags your requests with the IP address assigned to your home or access point. It allows the computer to make that connection to the internet and then granting you access to it. It is able to connect further through the use of internet protocols, which will be discussed later within this chapter.

This means that any time you connect to a new internet location, even from the same computer, you will be given a new IP address. The local wifi at the café will give you a different IP address than the one you have at home or at work, even if all three were accessed from the same computer. This is because, when you are on a new internet location, you are accessing the internet from a new location. Your information needs to take an entirely different route to reach you based on your location.

Public vs. Private IP address

IP addresses primarily come in two forms—public and private. Each of these is assigned in a slightly different way in order to allow for the necessary access to where they are supposed to go. The public IP address is the one discussed earlier—it is the one that is designed to allow access to the internet that is provided by the ISP. It is globally unique and can be discovered quite easily, either through commands in the terminal when using Linux systems or through the internet. Just searching "What is my IP address" online should provide your public IP address to you.

A private IP address acts similarly—it provides a computer a specific address, but in this case, it is used on computers within a private space or network without ever exposing that particular device. Think about a LAN—you may have several computers all on the same network. In this instance, the individual computers all hooked to your private network have private IP addresses. These IP addresses are not tied to the internet, but the connection point, likely a router, is able to send information to the right private IP address. The router, then, gets the public ID while the computers connected to the router get private ones.

Assigning an IP address

There is also a third type of IP address—the static IP address. This IP address will allow you to use various network services without needing to have the IP address of the system that is hosting the services.

This can be done in several ways, such as binding the MAC address to an IP address or in setting one up in a command line or a network manager.

When you wish to do this manually, you will need to look at the router that you are using. Generally speaking, routers will use their own methods to lock and bind IP addresses and you should always check the manual for the router that you are using. The way this works is by directly binding the MAC address to the IP address. The MAC address is the media access control address—it is an identifier that is put into a device, uniquely defining it. This is permanent and assigned to the network interface controller (NIC) for that particular device. This means that the item will always have the same MAC address, no matter how many times it is directly factory reset or altered.

When you make the IP address static, what you do is directly assign that one particular MAC address to one particular IP address. This method will not be used to create a static IP for a virtual machine, however.

In Kali Linux, creating a static IP address is incredibly simple. All you need to do is use the Network Manager settings. In doing so, you must go to the top right-hand corner of your screen and click on the menu arrow. Then, click on "Wired Connected" followed by "Wired Settings."

After you do this, you will be given a new window. You should see gear icons—click on the gear icon that is connected to the Wired menu. This will trigger another window to open, in which you will choose the IPv4 tab.

You can then shift the IPv4 method from automatic to manual, followed by entering the desired static IP that you would like to implement. When you are choosing out the desired address, keep in mind that the first seven digits of your chosen address should match the default gateway.

That is to say that if the router's gateway IP address is 123.456.7.8, your selected IP should have an address of 123.456.7.** and you should record that selected IP under Address under this menu.

You must also select your netmask—for most people, simply entering 255.255.255.0 is good enough. You must then record your Gateway, which should match the IP address of the router. This leads to the following settings:

Address	Netmask	Gateway
•123.456.7.10 •Uses the first 7 digits of the Gateway and chosen ending	•255.255.255.0 •This by default.	•123.456.7.8 •Also the IP of the router.

Upon lining up these settings, you can then choose to set any DNS settings if you want them, though this is not necessary. After finishing setting up the address, netmask, and gateway, you can hit apply.

In order to ensure that you have the router's IP address, all you need to do is enter the command:

---

ip ro

```
[Expert@msfihq:0]# ip ro
default via 94.76.122.153 dev eth3 proto 7
192.168.2.0/23 via 192.168.147.100 dev eth1 proto 7
192.168.111.0/24 via 192.168.147.100 dev eth1 proto 7
192.168.119.0/24 via 192.168.147.100 dev eth1 proto 7
192.168.120.0/23 via 192.168.147.100 dev eth1 proto 7
192.168.147.0/24 dev eth1 proto kernel scope link src 192.168.147.250
192.168.151.0/24 dev eth2 proto kernel scope link src 192.168.151.254
192.168.191.0/24 via 192.168.147.100 dev eth1 proto 7
192.168.197.0/24 via 192.168.147.100 dev eth1 proto 7
192.168.198.0/24 via 192.168.147.100 dev eth1 proto 7
192.168.199.0/24 via 192.168.147.100 dev eth1 proto 7
```

If you look after the response "default via," you will have your router's IP address.

Lastly, to then apply all of the changes to the IP address, you must restart the network. You can do so with the following command in the terminal:

---

sudo systemctl restart NetworkManager

Assuming you are already familiar with Linux and the basics behind using it, you know that sudo is the command that triggers the system to bypass any administrative restrictions, so long as you have been set as a sudo user. If you find that you are unfamiliar with this process, you may benefit from seeking out a beginner's guide to Linux before proceeding with the book.

With the sudo command entered, you can now stop to check your current local IP to make sure that your changes were received and made. You can do this with the following command

```
[Expert@msfihq:0]# ip a
1: lo: <LOOPBACK,PROMISC,DYNAMIC,NOTRAILERS,UP,LOWER_UP> mtu 65536 qdisc noqueue state UNKNOWN qlen 1000
    link/loopback 00:00:00:00:00:00 brd 00:00:00:00:00:00
    inet 127.0.0.1/8 scope host lo
       valid_lft forever preferred_lft forever
2: eth5: <BROADCAST,MULTICAST> mtu 1500 qdisc noop state DOWN qlen 1000
    link/ether 00:1c:7f:3d:a5:c2 brd ff:ff:ff:ff:ff:ff
3: eth1: <BROADCAST,MULTICAST,UP,LOWER_UP> mtu 1500 qdisc pfifo_fast state UP qlen 1000
    link/ether 00:1c:7f:3d:a5:c3 brd ff:ff:ff:ff:ff:ff
    inet 192.168.147.250/24 brd 192.168.147.255 scope global eth1
       valid_lft forever preferred_lft forever
    inet 192.168.147.254/24 brd 192.168.147.255 scope global secondary eth1:1
       valid_lft forever preferred_lft forever
4: eth6: <BROADCAST,MULTICAST> mtu 1500 qdisc noop state DOWN qlen 1000
    link/ether 00:1c:7f:3d:a5:c4 brd ff:ff:ff:ff:ff:ff
5: eth2: <NO-CARRIER,BROADCAST,MULTICAST,UP> mtu 1500 qdisc pfifo_fast state DOWN qlen 1000
    link/ether 00:1c:7f:3d:a5:c5 brd ff:ff:ff:ff:ff:ff
    inet 192.168.151.254/24 brd 192.168.151.255 scope global eth2
       valid_lft forever preferred_lft forever
6: eth7: <BROADCAST,MULTICAST> mtu 1500 qdisc noop state DOWN qlen 1000
    link/ether 00:1c:7f:3d:a5:c6 brd ff:ff:ff:ff:ff:ff
7: eth3: <BROADCAST,MULTICAST,UP,LOWER_UP> mtu 1500 qdisc pfifo_fast state UP qlen 1000
    link/ether 00:1c:7f:3d:a5:c7 brd ff:ff:ff:ff:ff:ff
    inet 94.76.122.154 /29 brd 94.76.122.159 scope global eth3
       valid_lft forever preferred_lft forever
8: Mgmt: <NO-CARRIER,BROADCAST,MULTICAST,UP> mtu 1500 qdisc pfifo_fast state DOWN qlen 1000
    link/ether 00:1c:7f:3d:a5:c8 brd ff:ff:ff:ff:ff:ff
    inet 192.168.200.208/27 brd 192.168.200.223 scope global Mgmt
       valid_lft forever preferred_lft forever
9: eth4: <BROADCAST,MULTICAST> mtu 1500 qdisc noop state DOWN qlen 1000
```

You should then be able to see what the IP address on your system is. If it matches what you have tried to set, then you have been successful in setting your own IP address.

Alternative, you can perform the following command:

---

ifconfig

```
[Expert@msfihq:0]# ifconfig
Mgmt        Link encap:Ethernet  HWaddr 00:1C:7F:3D:A5:C8
            inet addr:192.168.200.208  Bcast:192.168.200.223  Mask:255.255.255.224
            UP BROADCAST MULTICAST  MTU:1500  Metric:1
            RX packets:0 errors:0 dropped:0 overruns:0 frame:0
            TX packets:0 errors:0 dropped:0 overruns:0 carrier:0
            collisions:0 txqueuelen:1000
            RX bytes:0 (0.0 b)  TX bytes:0 (0.0 b)
            Interrupt:19 Memory:feae0000-feb00000

eth1        Link encap:Ethernet  HWaddr 00:1C:7F:3D:A5:C3
            inet addr:192.168.147.250  Bcast:192.168.147.255  Mask:255.255.255.0
            UP BROADCAST RUNNING MULTICAST  MTU:1500  Metric:1
            RX packets:120359636 errors:0 dropped:940 overruns:0 frame:0
            TX packets:112555911 errors:0 dropped:0 overruns:0 carrier:0
            collisions:0 txqueuelen:1000
            RX bytes:15850504096 (14.7 GiB)  TX bytes:87555236420 (81.5 GiB)
            Interrupt:17 Memory:fe4e0000-fe500000

eth1:1      Link encap:Ethernet  HWaddr 00:1C:7F:3D:A5:C3
            inet addr:192.168.147.254  Bcast:192.168.147.255  Mask:255.255.255.0
            UP BROADCAST RUNNING MULTICAST  MTU:1500  Metric:1
            Interrupt:17 Memory:fe4e0000-fe500000

eth2        Link encap:Ethernet  HWaddr 00:1C:7F:3D:A5:C5
            inet addr:192.168.151.254  Bcast:192.168.151.255  Mask:255.255.255.0
            UP BROADCAST MULTICAST  MTU:1500  Metric:1
            RX packets:0 errors:0 dropped:0 overruns:0 frame:0
            TX packets:0 errors:0 dropped:0 overruns:0 carrier:0
            collisions:0 txqueuelen:1000
            RX bytes:0 (0.0 b)  TX bytes:0 (0.0 b)
            Interrupt:19 Memory:fe6e0000-fe700000
```

Protocol Layers

As briefly touched upon earlier, the internet is run by protocols. This protocol has five distinct layers that come together to create an internet protocol stack. The first four layers of the internet protocol stack are contained within the TCI/IP model. In understanding how these layers work, you are able to see exactly how people and systems interact with the internet as a whole. This section will introduce you to the layers of the internet as well as the methods of accessing them.

Internet Protocol (IP)

The Internet Protocol (IP) is the primary protocol dictating how communications are managed over the internet. It explains how datagrams, the information that your computer sends when requesting further information, are relayed across networks and boundaries. Its primary function is routing information, which then allows for information to be transferred, which then creates the internet as a whole.

IP is tasked with transferring packets, small parcels of information that must be transmitted, from the source host to the destination host. It utilizes IP addresses in order to do so, providing them with the packets' headers. While the IP was once connectionless, it was also used as the basis of the Transmission Control Program that eventually became the Transmission Control Protocol (TCP). For this reason, you sometimes will see IP referred to as the TCP/IP, as will be discussed in the next section.

The IP began as IPv4 (Internet Protocol Version 4), though this is beginning to be replaced by IPv6.

Ultimately, the IP is responsible for several functions. It can be divided into four distinct functions—the application, transport, internet, and linking of data. There is a fifth layer to the transmission of data and packages as well—the physical layer, though the TCP/IP model does not encompass the physical.

The TCP/IP Model

The TCP/IP model is one of the specifications of IP—it is the definitive list of rules on how communication should occur between computers on a network. It dictates the formatting standard for data, allowing all systems to utilize the same standards. Essentially, the TCP/IP model allows for all systems, no matter where they originate from, to access the same internet.

This is done by creating standard datagrams—these datagrams have two components. They have a header and a payload.

	ISO/OSI		TCP/IP	
7	Application			
6	Presentation		Application	4
5	Session			
4	Transport		Transport	3
3	Network		Internet	2
2	Data Link		Network Access	1
1	Physical			

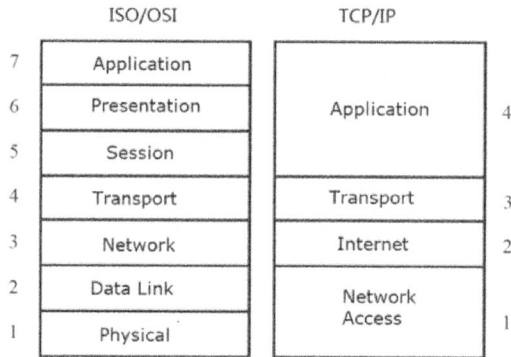

The header includes the source IP address, the IP address of the destination, and any other necessary metadata that will be needed to ensure that the information is all received exactly where it should be. The payload then is the data that will be delivered to the source that needs to receive it.

When the payload and the header are nested together into what is referred to as a packet, the process is known as encapsulation. With the IP stack, there are five distinct layers, as mentioned previously. The first four layers are relevant to the TCP/IP model. The first layer, the physical layer, is responsible for the encoding and transmission of data from one source to the proper network communications media.

It uses data that is referred to as bits that get sent from the physical layer, which the destination's physical layer will receive. Essentially, the first layer takes the input you put into the computer, through clicks and presses of your keyboard keys in bits and encodes them.

Next, you go through the data link layer—during this layer, the packets that were previously encoded are transferred from the network layer to two separate hosts. This transmission of packets is sometimes controlled by the software device driver in a network card or with firmware, and different protocols will have different methods of using this. In broadband internet, for example, access requires PPPoE as the necessary protocol, though a local wired network will utilize an Ethernet cord. Local wireless networks, on the other hand, will use IEEE 802.11 instead.

From the data link layer, you move on to the network or internet layer. This is where the data is actually taken from the source network and travels to the destination. It is typically achieved through passing the packet from network to network to network, a process referred to as internetwork, and this is where IP becomes relevant. This step involves data going from one source to the destination.

Once that data is sent to the destination, however, there are still two more layers before it can be accessed. The next layer is the Transport layer—its responsibility is to allow for the message to be transferred.

This usually occurs in one of two ways: either through transmission control protocol or through the User Datagram Protocol (UDP).

TCP as a system of communication refers to the connection-oriented communications protocol that is meant to allow for the exchange of messages across the internet. Usually deemed to be reliable thanks to the fact that there are several different error-checks to ensure that it all is translated and transmitted effectively. It is first ordered into packets and numbered, and then the information is sent to the recipient and requiring a response back to the sender to confirm receipt of the message in the first place. If the receiver's response is anything other than accurate, then the message gets resent properly to ensure that the right data and packets are sent in a way that is properly read. This is the most common form of communication and transmission of data across the internet.

UDP, on the other hand, allows for faster transmission of data. Unfortunately, the faster transmission of data comes at a cost—accuracy.

Error checking is done away with, and it instead focuses on sending data as quickly and accurately as possible. Because waiting for the submission of data can take time, latency, or lag between what has been requested and what has been done occurs. In some instances, people may prefer to sacrifice accuracy and security in favor of the speed of UDP. Both of these protocols work through developing beyond the IP protocol—they effectively are sending packets of information to an IP address that has been sent via TCP or UDP.

Threats to Network Security

Of course, with the creation of networks comes threats as well. Nothing good can be left free from harm or problems, and data and network security are no exception. Every addition of an extra source or node can lead to weaker links—there are more holes that could potentially be prodded into. There are more chances of failure. And that is exactly what those who break into networks, hacking them or exploiting them, are looking for. They can pose a serious threat to network security, and it is important to know and recognize that.

There are several different forms of hacking and attempts to exploit technology, and this section will address some of them. A few of these may sound familiar from the previous chapter, while others are new. These are still not an extensive list of all the ways that it is possible to exploit or hack into a system, though they are important to understand.

You cannot really understand networking if you do not understand the risk and threats as well.

Man-in-the-Middle

As discussed earlier in this book, the man-in-the-middle attack is an attack in which the attacker is secretly intercepting and sometimes altering the communication between a host and a recipient. The host and recipient think that they are able to communicate freely or that they are speaking directly with each other, but the MITM is listening—they are able to make two parties feel like they are safe and secure, all while gleaning valuable information that can be used later in some way, shape, or form.

This usually is done through the attacker managing to gain access to one of the transmission IDs that are meant to be unique between the two end users.

User

Original Connection

New Connection

Web Application

Attacker

Sometimes, this occurs when someone within the Wi-Fi range is able to manage to insert him or herself into the connection and begin to intercept information back and forth. It is the most successful when the attacker is able to successfully impersonate both endpoints, making sure that neither person or user has raised any suspicion.

Cyberattacks

Cyberattacks are intentional malicious attempts to steal information or otherwise breach an information system of another person. Typically, it occurs because someone sees some sort of value in deliberately interfering with someone else's computer or network. The reasons for cyberattacks have been growing lately, with people sometimes seeing them as instant crash grabs—they may intentionally hack into a system in order to ask for a ransom or to offer to fix the discovered exploit for a price. No matter the situation, these cyberattacks are undeniably damaging. They can have serious financial implications while also putting sensitive data at risk. This can happen either actively or passively.

An active cyberattack involves someone intentionally trying to get into a system for some reason or to get something. The hacker is deliberately attempting to make changes to the system for some reason to the data that is either going toward or away from the individual. These include the use of masquerade attacks, such as the pretending to be an individual that has greater privileges that are actually granted or authorized in the first place.

A passive cyberattack, on the other hand, occurs when a network system is monitored and scanned to find open vulnerabilities. Instead of attempting to change the information in some way or otherwise alter the network, the information is simply used to monitor the data in some way. It is taken for use, but is not actually altered.

This is what someone would do if they intended to leak important information in order to blackmail or reveal something that otherwise would have remained private. Think of a hacktivist who would willingly use this information in order to reveal something.

DOS and DDOS

A denial of service attack is an attack designed to cause serious problems to the network. The entire purpose of this is to flood a specific network in order to crash it. Just as a traffic jam builds up when too many people are on a road that is too small to accommodate for it, the network will not be able to manage too many requests at the same time if it is not large enough to do so. Usually, this is done with an attacker machine able to run a client program, which then constantly inundates the targeted server with pings and requests in order to cripple it. As the network continues to try to respond in time, the network slows and slows until it eventually just stops altogether.

DDOS (distributed denial of service) is exactly the same, though it makes use of several attacker machines rather than a single one. In doing so, larger networks can be compromised and crippled. Think about the implications of this happening—a website that needs to be functional will no longer be able to. A bank that has been crippled and cannot handle any traffic could risk people not being able to access funds.

A hospital system that is unable to access and manage their patients' information would be unable to access records and medical histories or see whether people have recently had access to their necessary medication or other treatments. This sort of attack can be absolutely devastating, depending on the context.

MAC Spoofing

As you have already read, MAC addresses are usually permanent and hard-coded onto the NIC of a device. However, there are ways that this can be edited and altered.

This is known as MAC spoofing. When MAC spoofing is used, the operating system being targeted or interacted with is able to be fooled to believe that the MAC address is actually something entirely different. Effectively, this allows for the identity of a computer to be altered and hidden. This is most often done because the individual wants to bypass the access control lists. If they have been banned from a server, for example, they are able to bypass this list by changing it. They can also impersonate another device in order to gain unauthorized access to a system through similar means.

MAC spoofing can also be done to conceal identity—if you wish to use an unencrypted connection, such as an IEEE encrypted line, you are not going to be able to prevent the Wi-Fi network from providing others with access to the MAC address. When you spoof your address, you are able to avoid being traceable. You will have hidden that identity and in doing so, you are able to be invisible, so to speak. Your true MAC address has been concealed and because of that, you can escape detection by law enforcement.

CHAPTER 3
Kali Linux: The Hacker Operating System

At this point, you should be able to see that cybersecurity is crucial and that there are very good reasons for learning how to both hack in order to identify any weak links in your systems and to protect them from harm. This is where Kali Linux comes in. Now, as a quick disclaimer before continuing, it is never recommended that you use these methods to deliberately damage or sabotage someone else or their connection. You should not be using the tools within Kali Linux for illegal purposes. However, if you do choose to do so, keep in mind that you will be entirely responsible for your own actions. This book does not condone, nor does it encourage the use of hacking for nefarious purposes. If you do decide to utilize these skills, the reason for doing so should be that you wish to protect or defend your own security.

This chapter will introduce you to Kali Linux properly—you will learn about what Linux is first and foremost, and from there, you will learn about Kali Linux, the specific distribution of Linux. You will be taught how to install Kali Linux, what Kali Linux comes packaged with, and some of the common Kali Linux specific information and commands that you may need to know. By the end of this chapter, you will have a working knowledge of what Kali Linux is as well as how to install it into your computer.

What is Linux?

First, you must understand what Linux itself is, as Kali Linux is ultimately a Linux distribution (colloquially referred to as a distro). If you are already familiar with Linux, you can skip this section, as it is not likely to provide you with anything else. If you are unfamiliar with Linux, please read through this section and remember that this is not a distribution to be taken lightly or to be treated as a toy. Kali Linux is dangerous and should not be in the hands of someone who is going to be unable to protect against serious damages.

Linux itself is an operating system—it is designed to be open-source. This means that the code itself is readily alterable and free to distribute. It is intentionally designed to be flexible and able to be changed in several different ways.

The code is open-source, meaning access to altering the mainframe and base code is quite simple, and in many forms of Linux, if you are simply able to gain access to the terminal, you will be able to tell it to do anything—even if what you tell it to do is detrimental or risks crashing the entire system that you have installed.

When you learn to use Linux, you are given free control over the system. More specifically, however, Linux describes the kernel itself rather than the actual operating system. The kernel is the base that allows for the computer's OS to start up the hardware, allowing for the initial interaction between OS and user to begin building from that. Some forms of Linux, such as Mint or Ubuntu, are designed to be readily accessible, easily understood, and built to be managed and utilized with ease.

Other distributions of Linux are far more technical and require you to have much more programming knowhow in order to truly command them. These are distributions such as Gentoo, which is widely known as an internet meme much like deleting System 34 in Windows in order to cause the whole thing to crash. Other forms still bring with them several tools and functions that you may not necessarily have access to otherwise, such as several of the penetration-based tools of Kali Linux. It is important for you to understand what you can and cannot do, what your own capabilities are, and how you can possibly interact with the systems before you make it a point to install Kali Linux.

If thus far, you were lost with the talk of kernels and distributions or the idea of coding your own programs and commanding your computer, please stop reading now and seek out a beginner's book before revisiting. These concepts are crucial and it is expected that you have some level of familiarity with the system from here on out, whether you are a beginner or not. Remember that you can cause irreparable harm if you attempt to use this system without knowing fully what you are doing—you must be cautious and careful to avoid a disaster of your own doing.

What is Kali Linux?

Kali Linux is a specifically Debian-based Linux distribution. Developed by Offensive Security, Kali Linux was designed to be a leading trainer in information security professionals. With the tools utilized in Kali Linux, you are able to begin hacking with relative ease if you know what you are doing—it brings with it several of the tools that you will find necessary, and it also allows for training and certification.

In fact, if you wish to be an information security technician or professional, you are most likely going to be required to have a certification that you have earned based upon the courses taught by Offensive Security.

When you have used Kali Linux, you are gaining access to the tools that are designed to help you with information security tasks. You will be able to engage in Penetration Testing, security research and more. Because Kali Linux is managed and maintained by Offensive Security, one of the leading trainers in cybersecurity, you know that the tools provided are much like the ones that you will be fighting in the future.

In particular, this distribution of Linux is designed to meet the needs of penetration testing professionals—because it is aimed toward professionals, it assumes that you already are familiar with Linux as an operating system. Kali Linux boasts several important traits that make it useful in the hacking world—these tools make it valuable to both those interested in hacking for nefarious purposes and those who are interested in bettering security overall. However, these traits came at a cost. Several of the commonly known benefits to using Linux distros in the first place have been changed in order to make Kali Linux a more valuable tool. After all, the beauty of Linux is that it is capable of anything that you are capable of programming so you are able to create an operating system that exactly serves the needs you have. Now, let's take a moment to go over those key changes from the standard Linux distribution.

It is single user root access.

Remember, root access refers to whether or not someone has administrative authority on that device. The root user has no safeguards, is not told any under any circumstances, and cannot be overridden by the system. In most cases with various other Linux systems, it is strongly recommended that you avoid using the root access account and instead set up another with sudo privileges.

However, that is not possible with Kali Linux—the OS does not allow for any other users or for root access to be left behind. This means that the operating system if you do not know what you are doing, can be completely destroyed with just one or two typos or not knowing what you are doing. Because of the nature of the tools and usage scenario with Kali Linux, almost everything you will be doing would be considered higher privilege and you would either have to constantly sudo command the system, or you would need to remain in the root user account anyway.

Because having to avoid the root account would be a burden, Kali Linux has instead shifted over to remain in root access constantly. This is yet another reason that this is not a distro for a beginner.

Kali Linux

- Single user root access
- Network services are disabled
- Linux kernel is custom and patched for wireless injection
- Repositories list is minimal for security

Network services are disabled.

While network services are usually enabled in Linux distros, within Kali Linux, there are system hooks that leave network services disabled by default. This is a security method—it allows for services to remain secure and protects the distribution regardless of the packages that are installed. Other forms of networking, such as Bluetooth, are also disabled.

Linux kernel is customized.

While nearly every other Linux distribution is linked together by the common Linux kernel, the Kali Linux distro does not use that exact kernel—the one that is utilized in Kali Linux has been customized, allowing it to be patched for wireless injection, yet another way that it is able to act as a tool useful for penetration testing.

Repositories list is minimal.

Because Kali Linux is designed to be secure, there is a minimal list of sources for software that are allowed access to the system. While many people may feel the need or temptation to add systems that are not authorized or on the repository list, doing so can cause a high likelihood of crashing the Linux installation altogether. For this reason, you must recognize that Kali Linux is not so much a day-to-day OS as a tool to use for training and very specific usage scenarios. If you do not make use of it in one of these scenarios, such as penetration testing or practicing your skills, you are going to find little use for the system. You will not be using this for daily web browsing and attempting to answer emails or play video games—attempting to do so runs the risk of crashing the whole thing.

Should I use Kali Linux?

You may expect that a book written about Kali Linux would be spouting out all of the reasons that you should, in fact, use this distribution. However, due to the risks, the specialized and unique nature of this distribution, and the limitations that come with it, it is important to walk through the reasons that Kali Linux is likely not for you instead.

This distribution is designed specifically for professional testers and specialists. It is difficult to learn and it will not give you access to do anything you want.

Despite being open-access, it is only so open—there are aspects of this distribution that are locked due to security reasons, and you will not be able to change them. The packages in repositories, for example, must be signed by the committee, and these repositories are upstream. It is well-tested and the development team is one that can be trusted and respected. However, if you want a system that you have complete access to, Kali Linux is not for you.

Yes, there is some degree of customizability, but you will not be able to install juts anything. You must install from a chosen list of repositories if you wish to have them work right away.

If you try to install something not on that list, you will have to go through several hoops to try to fix it up, and even then, you still are quite likely to cause more problems than you have fixed. For regular browsing and usage, Kali Linux is not right for you.

If you are already familiar with Linux and already are comfortable with network administration or system administration and want a tool to learn more, this may be the right OS, but this should never be treated as the first intro to Linux. Especially because any unauthorized attempts to penetrate a network can not only cause significant damage but also carry hefty legal or personal issues, this should only be used by people that know what they are doing and are not likely to accidentally destroy someone else's network or access to service. Again, because it is so crucial to reiterate, if you are a beginner, seek out a Linux distribution that is designed to be easier—Ubuntu, Mint, and Debian are all fantastic starting points.

Of course, if you are a penetration tester already or are actively studying penetration in order to become certified, Kali Linux is exactly right for you. You cannot beat the tools that are designed by professionals for professionals, nor can you beat the price of free for that toolset.

Kali Linux Features

If you have decided that Kali Linux is may be right for you, there are several tools that may be relevant to you. This section will guide you through the most common features of Kali Linux so you can begin to understand better whether this will be good for you to use.

Hundreds of Penetration Testing Tools

Kali Linux boasts a massive repository of tools that can be used for penetration testing, all of which have been verified and tested to be safe. Every tool provides a purpose that will be useful to your work in penetrating and controlling systems.

Free

This is perhaps one of the most compelling reasons to make use of Kali Linux—if it serves the right uses for you, it is absolutely free. You will never be required to pay to have access to this set of tools, meaning that there are no ongoing licenses to maintain.

Secure

Kali Linux has been developed by a small group that is trusted to interact with the repositories and even that has several protocols to help make sure that Kali Linux is as secure as possible. This means that any package that will be sent for download will be signed by developers who have committed and built it, allowing for tracking accountability if anything were to go wrong.

Customizable

While Kali Linux has very specific usage scenarios that are encouraged, and certain usages of the system are strongly frowned upon, the entire system has been built to be customizable. You can try to change Kali Linux to suit your needs, even if those needs go against the recommended usage. You may run into complications, but you are able to attempt to do whatever you think you need to do.

Customizable

Unlike many other penetration tools, Kali Linux allows for true multilingual support. Instead of having to operate and learn everything in English, people are able to use Kali Linux in their own native language.

Open Source Git Tree

All source code is available for people to see or tweak to their specific needs. People can follow the development and source codes to make sure that they can get exactly what they want and need, with the few limitations listed in the previous section.

FHS Compliant

Kali Linux allows for Linux users to locate their files and libraries thanks to the familiar Filesystem Hierarchy Standard that has always been used. This means that if you are already familiar with Linux, using this has one less hurdle to get over.

Wireless Device Support

Kali Linux has been designed to support a wide range of wireless devices, allowing for it to be compatible with USB and other wireless devices with ease. This allows for easier access to information and transmission of information.

Custom Kernel

Because penetration testers need to be able to do wireless assessments, the Linux kernel within Kali will always be up to date with all of the latest patches to aid in the act of injection to other systems.

How to Install Kali Linux

Now, you should have a good idea of whether installing Kali Linux will benefit you. If you think that it is, in fact, what is right for you after having looked through everything about the OS, then it is time to begin discussing the installation process of the OS. Installation is the first step toward being able to utilize the Kali Linux operating system and can be done in several ways. If you are installing Kali Linux in any way that is not traditional installation method of installing the Kali Linux OS on your computer or if you think that you will be running a virtual machine, you may be better off going to the official Kali Linux site and looking at the guides and tutorials that they have available.

What You Need for Installation

When you are ready to install, you must make sure that you have everything that you need. This can vary greatly depending on the system that you are using. Those running Linux probably already have everything that they need installed, but if you are running either macOS X or Windows, you are going to need to make sure you install the proper GPG for your particular operating system.

Either way, if you go to the Kali Linux Kali Docs Official Documentation library, you will be able to go to the instructions for downloading the official Kali Linux images. Toward the bottom of the page, both links are provided for you to download the prover version of GPG.

After installing GPG, you need to download and import your copy of the official Kali Linux key. You will do this with the following command:

```
$ wget -q -O - https://archive.kali.org/archive-key.asc | gpg --import
```

In response, you will be provided with a key number. In order to verify that your key has been installed, you must try one more command:

```
$ wget -q -O gpg --fingerprint
44C6513A8E4FB3D30875F758ED444FF07D8D0BF6
```

So long as you do not run into anything telling you there is an error, you should see that you have a key as well as a time limit during which the key is effective.

Step 1: Getting official Kali Linux images

When you are installing your OS, you need an ISO file—this requires you to have a USB drive or a hard disk or some other method of interacting with the computer that you are installing Kali Linux on. You will need to have the image in either 32-bit or 64-bit format depending on the architecture of the system that you are using. When you need to know what system you are running and are currently on either Linux or OS X, you can enter a command in the terminal to get the result.

You will enter in:

---

uname –m

---

and after doing so, you will get the response of either "x86_64," meaning that you are running a 64-bit format at the moment, or a response of "i386" meaning that you are currently running a 32-bit system. You need to make sure that the ISO that you choose is the right version.

On a Windows 10 system, you will need to press the **Start** button, followed by selecting **Settings > About**. In opening up the settings, you should see device specifications in the right.

There, you should be able to see whether your system is running either a 32-bit or 64-bit system.

You will be able to get the proper image in either .iso/.img files or in .torrent files. Keep in mind that doing so is specific to an Intel-based PC. You also have access to files that will allow you to run Kali Linux on a virtual machine, or in other formats as well. When you are downloading Kali Linux, make sure that you are always doing so from the Kali Linux official site run by Operational Security. Doing anything other than that can lead to serious problems as you no longer have a guarantee that the installation that you are currently running is safe and secure. You will need to ensure that the file you are downloading is secure if you are going to be using it to penetration test your own personal systems.

Step 2: Verify the Kali Image

Before going so far as to run Kali Linux Live, which will be discussed shortly, you need to double-check that you have the legitimate, official release of Kali Linux instead of some sort of hacked or altered version that was distributed elsewhere on the internet. You can do this quite simply in one of three different ways:

- Download an ISO image from the official Kali Linux "downloads" mirror and then calculate the SHA256 has while comparing it to the one listed on the Kali Linux site. You should be able to do this quite simply—but this is also potentially vulnerable to exploits.

- Download the ISO image through a torrent and it will also give you a file that has the calculated SHA256 signature on it. You are then able to use the shasum command if you are already on Linux or OSX , or in a tool on Windows to verify that the file's signature matches the signature within that other folder downloaded. Again, this suffers from potentially being vulnerable to exploit as someone could quite simply provide you with matching numbers just to make it look like a legitimate installation of Kali Linux in order to ensure that you are fooled.

- The only way to be as certain as possible is a bit more involved—you will need to download the cleartext signature file and the version of the file that was signed off with the official private key. Then, you must utilize GNU Privacy Guard. This will then verify that the SHA256 combination and the one in the cleartext files match, and then it will ensure that the signed version of the file with the SHA256 hash is also correctly signed with the proper official key.

Step 3: Create Kali Linux Bootable USB Drive

Perhaps the fastest method of getting Kali up and running is through using a live bootable USB. Essentially, what you are doing is getting Kali Linux onto a USB drive and then booting it up from that USB. This comes with several advantages of its own, such as avoiding any sort of destruction or mayhem. When you use this, you are not making any changes to the system you are using—you are simply running it from the USB. This also brings up the point that it is portable and customizable—you will be able to take it with you anywhere and boot up from any computer, and you will be able to create your own custom Kali ISO onto the USB drive in the same way that will be discussed here.

In order to create the bootable drive, you will need to have a verified copy of the ISO, a disk imager utility (if you are using Windows, you can download the Win32 Disk Imager, or if you are on Linux or OS X, you likely already have this and all you will need to do is use the command, dd in order to pull it up) and a USB drive or an SD card, so long as the system that you are using allows for direct access with either of those methods. Your storage should have at least 4GB with more recommended.

Step 3.A: Create the Bootable USB with Windows

When you do this on a Windows computer, you will have several steps to go through that are different compared to if you had been running a Linux or OS X machine.

- Attach the USB drive into any available USB port on the computer and note whichever drive designator has been set to it. With it mounted, launch Win32.

- Select the Kali Linux ISO file that you are imaging and confirm that you are overriding the proper USB drive. When you have confirmed that it is correct, press the Write button. As soon as it is finished imaging, eject the USB drive and it is now ready to use.

Step 3.B: Creating the Bootable USB with Linux

On Linux, the steps are slightly more involved, and you run the risk of struggling or accidentally overwriting a disk drive that was unintended. You are going to need to make sure that you are using the right commands to guarantee that you are not accidentally overwriting anything.

- First, you must figure out the device path that you will be using to write the image to the USB drive. You want to do this without the USB inserted at that point in time. Within the terminal, you want to write:

---

sudo fdisk –l

You should get an output that shows a single drive with three partitions.

- At this point, plug in your USB to the available port and once again repeat the previous command of sudo fdisk -l and you should now get a similar output showing an extra device this time that was not there before—this time, that is your USB drive.

- Now, you must image the ISO file onto the USB device with a command similar to the one that will be provided below. This command assumes that your ISO image is named "kali-linux-2017.1-amd64.iso" and is currently within the working directory. It also assumes that your USB drive's name is "/dev/sdb" and you will want to replace the name of the file and the name of the drive if necessary. You can choose the blocksize if you wish to try to speed things up, but this is the safest size that has created reliable images.

The command here is:

```
dd if=kali-linux-2017.1-amd64.iso of=/dev/sdb bs=512k
```

- The imaging process can take upwards and sometimes over 10 minutes, so be patient as you wait for this process. You will not get any feedback about this process until the system is done.

- When it is finished, your USB device is now ready to boot.

Step 3.C: Creating a Bootable USB on OS X

- Start with the USB drive unplugged. Open the Terminal and type the command:

```
diskutil list
```

- You should see several device paths, just as with the Linux version. You will get information on each of the partitions and all of the information that you could possibly need.

- Now, plug in the USB device and rerun diskutil list again. Doing so will now present you with a new disk drive. You can now see a new disk drive that was not present before, which is how you now know how to address the command.

- Now, unmount the drive—this time, we will act as if the drive is named "/dev/disk6" for the example. Your command will be something like:

---

diskutil unmount /dev/disk6

- At this point, you need to image the Kali ISO file to the device with a command such as:

---

sudo dd if=kali-linux-2017.1-amd.iso of=/dev/disk6 bs=1m

Keep in mind that there is no guarantee that your own file and drive will have the same file names. You will need to change them accordingly. Again, there will be no feedback until the drive is done loading, at which point you will have a bootable USB.

Now, you will be able to use any of your USB drives to boot up the OS. All you need to do is bring up the boot menu upon starting your computer with the USB mounted and make sure you select Kali Linux. There are other methods that you can use to access Kali Linux, such as installing it onto your computer itself, but one of the most recommended methods of accessing the software is through the use of the USB drive. If you have an interest in downloading the entire system onto your hardware, feel free to browse around the specific Kali Linux official website for more access and information to do exactly that.

CHAPTER 4
Basic Linux Commands

From this point on, the information you will be getting is a mix of practical information and information that you can actively use in some way. This chapter in particular will provide you with the necessary information to begin interacting with Kali Linux. You will be given a list of the most common and basic commands necessary.

As you read through these commands, try to really familiarize yourself with them. You want to make sure you understand what they are and how they can be best used to benefit you. If you are able to do so, you will ensure that you are also able to interact with your Linux distribution, no matter which you have chosen. Remember that with Kali Linux, you will be in root user by default and you will need to take the necessary precautions. When using several of these commands when you do not have root access, you run into problems that stop you from being able to move forward. However, with Kali, if you are already in the root user, the command is instantly carried out, even if it is a harmful one.

This is why attention to detail, and a meticulous amount of it, is crucial if you really want to develop your skills with Kali Linux and become skilled at penetration testing and hacking.

The Terminal

If you are familiar with Linux and basic commands, you should also be familiar with the Terminal. This is the way that you are able to interact with the shell of Linux, commanding it to do what you expect. You are essentially going to be putting in input to the server and then expecting it to come out the other end with the proper response. This is the basis of the simplest Linux commands.

As a quick refresher, if it has been a while, you will be emulating the terminal in a graphical environment so you can see the input and output in a way that you can read and understand. If you already have Linux or OS X, you already have access to Terminal, and you can also install others. If you have Windows, you may want to install PuTTY. Kali Linux will also have its own terminal within it as well that you are able to access with ease.

Command Prompts

When you are interacting with the Terminal, you are using command prompts or shell prompts—you will likely see these used interchangeably as you read through various guides. When you are within the terminal, there is a very specific composition of the prompt that you will see. It will be the username of the user, the hostname of the server, the directory you are in, and the prompt symbol. In most cases, the prompt symbol that you will see is **$**.

Effectively, then, if you are nicknamed hacker as your user, and your server that you are on is hacking and you are currently in the default home directory, you may see a default prompt of:

hacker@hacking:~$

In Kali Linux, however, you are always logged onto the single root user account. You are going to see the username of "root" instead of "hacker" or any other name that may have been there.

Executing the Commands

When you want to give your commands then, you must specify what you want in a fashion that the system is able to manage properly.

You can enter a script, a series of prescribed information that will trigger the system to respond in a specific way. You can also enter your own commands instead. This is what the majority of this current chapter will be: ways to interact and command the server.

When a command is running, it is called a process. When that process is happening in the foreground, you must wait for it to finish before you can do anything else. This is the default way to run the program.

You can also enter your commands in two forms: With or without arguments. When you enter a command without an argument, you are entering a simple command without expecting anything else. This will cause the computer to send you to exactly what you have specified or done exactly what you said. If you write **ls**, for example, you will suddenly get everything listed out in front of you on the screen—the current directory's files and directories.

However, an argument seeks to alter that command somewhat. In adding an argument, you add an extra condition—you may tell your system to bring up the files of a different directory. You may tell your system to shut down in 30 minutes instead of instantly. They add a change to the meaning of the original command. When you enter a command with arguments, you will enter it in a specific order of command, then the specification or location of what you are running.

Another common way that commands are executed is with options—this means that they have some sort of modification to follow. This is followed by a - and a letter that tells the system what you need from it. For example, if we go back to **ls**, you may choose to add something else to it, such as **ls -l** which tells your system that you want it to list out a longer list of permission, including far more details than would ordinarily be included.

You can also mix and match, so you can have your options and arguments combined—in fact, it is incredibly common to mix the two together in order to run the right command.

From here on, you will be provided with several commands within Linux that you will find to be useful. These will either be a great refresher course, or you did not need this information in the first place. If you did not need this information, or you feel confident in your ability to navigate a Linux system, feel free to drop off here and skip to the next chapter. However, if you are not entirely confident in your ability to navigate through your software, it may be smart to at least spend the time to read over this comprehensive list of commands that have been provided for you.

Of course, you can also always come back to this information later if you ever feel like you need a command and want to make sure that you are able to really learn how to use them.

Archives

The codes within this section are related specifically to the archive files within your system. They will help you to interact directly with archives, whether to access, move, or otherwise interact with them.

tar cf archive.tar directory

> This will create a tar file (archive.tar) that contains the directory.

tar cjf archive.tar.bz2 directory

> Similar to above, but the tar file will be compressed using the bzip2 format.

tar czf archive.tar.gz directory

> Another variation of the first command. It will create a gzip-compressed tar (archive.tar.gz).

tar xf archive.tar

> This is the opposite command of the above. It will extract the data from archive.tar.

tar xjf archive.tar.bz2

> Use this to extract data from a bzip2 compressed tar

tar xzf archive.tar.gz

> The command to extract from a tar that was compressed under the gzip format.

Directory Navigation

These codes will allow you access to moving around the directory quickly and easily. When you do this, you are able to shift around from space to space without having to manually go through your directories yourself one at a time.

It is easier to go through hit with the directory navigation.

cd

> You will be moved to the HOME directory

cd..

> It looks similar to the above, but has two periods. Will move you one level up the directory tree. For example, you are in directory 2, which lies within directory 1. You will move to directory 1 with this command.

cd /etc

> You will move to the /etc directory.

Disk Usage

These particular commands are directly related to disk usage. They will allow you to see all sorts of information about your current disk status, which can be incredibly necessary when you are monitoring your system closely.

df -h

You will be able to see the used and available space on your disks with this command.

df -i

Use this to see used and available inodes on your (mounted) filesystems.

du -ah

Will bring up file size for all objects and directories in a human-readable format (bytes, megabytes, gigabytes).

du -sh

Similar to the above, but will display the only the information from the directory currently being worked in.

fdisk -l

When you need to see the partition sizes and types of your hard disks, use this command.

File and Directory Commands

The commands within this section will help you interact directly with the file and directory within your system. They will allow you all sorts of extra access and usability of your files and allow you to get the most out of your system and efficiency.

cp fileA fileB

This command will copy over file A over to file B.

cp -r source_directory destination

The command will copy over the directory recursively over to a selected destination. If the location already exists, the directory will be copied over. If the location does not exist, it will be created with a copy of the source directory files

ls -al

Command will list all the files in a directory in a detailed format.

mv fileA fileB

Renames fileA to fileB. It can also move a file. If fileB is a directory, the command will move fileA into said directory.

mkdir directory

Makes a new directory.

pwd

Displays the directory you are currently in.

rm file

Removes the file in question. Most commonly known as deleting a file.

rm -f file

"Forces" the deletion of a file. No confirmation prompt will follow, so be sure you intend to delete this file

rm -r directory

Deletes a directory, along with its contents recursively

rm -rf directory

Use this when you want to "force" the deletion of a directory and its contents recursively. Again, be sure this is what you intend to do, as no confirmation will be asked.

File Transfers

These commands act as your guide to moving around files from place to place as necessary in order to ensure that you are always able to put your files where you want them.

rsync -a /home /backups/

Will synchronize the home directory over to /backups/ home.

rsync -avz /home server:/backups/

> Compression enabled synchronization of files or directories between a local and remote system.

scp file.txt server:/tmp

> Secure copies the file (in this case file.txt) to the /tmp folder on the server.

scp -r server:/var/www /tmp

> Recursively copies all directories and files from the server to the current system's /tmp directory.

scp server:/var/www/*.html /tmp

> Copies overall .html files from the server to the local /tmp directory.

Hardware Information Commands

These commands will provide you with all sorts of information about your hardware, ensuring that your hardware is functioning properly and effectively so you can be sure that all is well with your system.

badblocks -s /dev/sda

> This will check to see if there are any unreadable blocks on the disk sda (you can change sda to whatever disk drive you want to check).

cat /proc/cpuinfo

This will provide you with the current CPU information, such as usage, speed, and other important aspects of its ability to run.

cat /proc/meminfo

This will provide you with memory information, such as usage, speed, and other important aspects of its ability to run.

dmidecode

This will show you pertinent hardware information from the BIOS.

dmesg

This will show messages in the kernel ring buffer.

lspci -tv

This shows you the current PCI devices.

lsusb -tv

This shows your current USB devices.

free -h

This will display the free and used memory space in your system at that moment, specifically in a human-readable form. You can also select to -m instead of -h for the display in MB, or -g to get your result in GB.

hdparm –I /dev/sda

This will provide you with all sorts of information about the disk sda.

Installing Packages

These commands are all about installing packages from your files, whether from zip files, downloaded files, or otherwise.

rpm -i package.rpm

Installs the package from a local file, in this case named package.rpm.

make install

As opposed to installing from a package, this will have you install software from source.

yum info package

Displays information about the package you reference.

yum install package

Installs a package.

yum remove package

Uninstalls (removes) a package.

yum search keyword

Provides a search for a package using a keyword

Networking

These commands are directly related to networking—allowing you to see what is going on with your own network and anything that your own network is interacting with.

dig domain

Displays the DNS information for a given domain.

dig -x IP_ADDRESS

Use this to run a reverse lookup of a given IP address.

ethtool eth0

A tool to view and change network drivers and hardware settings.

host domain

Displays the DNS IP address for a given domain.

hostname -i

This command is used to displaying the network address of the "host name".

hostname -I

Very similar to the above command, but this will display all local ip addresses.

ifconfig -a

This will bring up all network interfaces and their ip addresses.

ifconfig eth0

Will display the eth0 address and its details.

netstat -nutlp

Will show oyu any listening tcp & udp ports and their related programs.

ping host

Will send an ICMP echo request to "host"

wget http://domain.com/file

Downloads the web file found at the given web address.

whois domain

Will display the whois information for "domain".

Performance Monitoring

These commands are dedicated to ensuring that you are able to monitor your system's performance. This will make sure that your system is functioning well, effectively, and to your preference in order to ensure that there is nothing further you have to do to optimize your own settings to what you want or need them to be.

htop

This will allow you to move to the top of the process viewer.

iostat 1

This will allow you to see the input/output statistics.

lsof

Allows for a list of all open files currently presents on the system.

lsof -u [username]

Allows for a list of open files present currently by the username specified.

mpstat 1

This will allow you to see processor-related stats.

tail 100 var/log/messages

This will let you see the last 100 system log messages.

tcpdump –i eth0

This will allow you to see all packets on that particular interface listed (in this case, eth0).

tcpdump –i eth0 'port 10'

This will allow for the monitoring of data on port 10, and you can change the port name to whichever port you are trying to manage.

top

This will show the top processes and allow you to manage them.

vmstat 1

This will allow you to see the virtual memory-related statistics.

Process Management

These commands are dedicated to process management—they tell you what the processes that are currently ongoing are doing, as well as allow you to shift from foreground processes to background processes as needed to make sure that your own activity does not suffer due to other processes running as well.

bg

> Will show background tasks or those that have stopped.

fg

> This command will push the most recent background process to the foreground.

fg n

> Similar to the above command, this will push process "n" to the front

kill pid

> Use this to end or "kill" a particular process, where the process ID matches "pid".

killall processname

> When you want to kill all processes with a particular name, utilize this command.

ps

> Displays your own processes currently running.

ps -ef

> Displays all of the processes currently running in the system.

ps -ef | grep processname

> This will display the information for "processname".

Search

When you need to find something within your system, these commands are your best bet. When you are using your search commands, you will be able to find the files you need quick access to with ease and learn exactly where they are so you are able to jump to them and access them elsewhere.

find /home -size +25M

Utilize this command to find files larger than 25MB in / home

find /home/mark -name 'prefix*'

This will find files in /home/mark that start with "prefix".

grep pattern file

This will look for pattern in "file".

grep -r pattern directory

Performs a recursive search for pattern in "directory".

locate name

Will look for files and directories by the specified "name".

SSH Logins

ssh host

Connects to host using the username you use locally.

ssh user@host

Connects to host as "user".

ssh -p port user@host

> Connects to host using port.

System Information Commands

These commands are all used for some sort of system information to understand what the system is doing and how you are able to interact with it. These are Linux specific—they should work for any form of Linux you are operating within, Kali Linux included.

Some of these commands may be less useful on Kali Linux, but they are important to know anyway when interacting with other Linux systems. Consider this your sort of refresher course on how to interact with Linux.

cal

> This will show you the current month's calendar.

cat /etc/redhat-release

> This shows you which redhat is currently present on your computer for use.

date

> This will show you the current time and date on the system you are using.

hostname

This will tell you what the name of the system host is.

hostname -I

Will provide you with the host's IP address.

last reboot

This will show you the last time that the system was rebooted.

uname -a

This allows for the display of the Linux system's information that is stored.

uname -r

This allows for the output to show which kernel release you are using.

uptime

Tells you how long your system has been up or how long it has been loading.

w

This will show you who is currently online on the system.

whoami

This will tell you who you are currently logged into the system as.

User Information and Management Commands

These commands are crucial to your ability to managing user information. When you master these controls, you can add and remove people from your server. You can make sure that certain people have certain permissions, and more. These commands may not be so necessary within Kali Linux, where you are designed to be in root user and not others, they are still fantastic to know and understand.

groupadd group1

Allows you to create a new group "group1" in this instance. You can replace "group1 with any other name for your group.

id

shows the user and group ids of the current user on the system.

last

Shows who the last people that logged on were.

useradd –c "full name" –m "nickname"

Allows for the creation of an account with the comment of "full name" and the home directory of "nickname".

userdel "name"

allows you to delete the user "name".

usermod –aG group1 "name"

Allows you to move user "name" to the "group1" group.

PART TWO

Kali Linux

Hacking

CHAPTER 5
Nmap - Detecting and Exploiting Vulnerabilities

A t this point, you may be quite eager to get started with Kali Linux once and for all. You should now have the OS installed yourself, or you are preparing to do so. Either way, reading through this section can provide you with valuable information. This is where you begin to see the true power of Kali Linux and how it can be used. You will begin to see the strength that can be earned in hacking and in learning to see and wield that strength for yourself, you should also be able to begin to see just how easy it is for a network to go unprotected or undefended. When this happens, it is in your best interest to ensure that you can figure out vulnerabilities in order to patch them up. Nmap is just one of many tools that Kal Linux offers, and this particular chapter focuses on it.

Nmap is powerful, allowing you to gather and identify information that is meant to be useful, allowing you to detect everything on the system. It is primarily a security tool, but you should keep in mind that it can be used to cause harm as well.

Now, it is time to dive into the beginning of the actual hacking process. If you have already installed Kali Linux, go ahead and open it up—Nmap comes by default, already provided within the system.

What is Nmap?

Nmap stands for network mapper—it is an incredibly popular tool that is used to discover that is available to you. As with all of the tools provided to you within the Kali Linux distribution, this is free to use and secure. When you use Nmap, you are able to map out networks, allowing yourself to see inventories and find open ports as well. It is quite simple to use—it brings up a terminal that you are able to enter your commands and scripts within, allowing you to do whatever you would like within the system once you have gotten in. This tool is able to work through firewalls and routers, it can bypass an IP filter, and it is able to navigate into systems. While it was designed to be capable of getting through massive networks, it can also be used on smaller scales as well. It is primarily used for port scanning, version detection, operating system detection, and using ping sweeps. It works quite simply—it uses IP packets in order to find hosts on a network and what they are running. Plenty of information can be earned just by finding out what someone's computer is running on. Overall, Nmap is incredibly powerful—it enables you to do all sorts of actions and search for several exploits. It not only gathers information but also allows for the scanning of security, making it a multipurpose tool that can greatly benefit you. It can be used for actions such as:

- Detecting any live hosts on a network
- Detecting any open ports that are currently present on the host
- Detecting vulnerability through Nmap script
- Detecting OS, hardware, and software

The tool itself is incredibly common and it is also compatible both with CLI and GUI, meaning it is not only common and powerful, but also flexible.

How to Use Nmap to Understand and Exploit Vulnerabilities

When you are ready to use Nmap, you have several different options. You will be able to scan one target, limited targets, or several targets, all based on the command that you are able to submit. The target determines exactly how you would go through the process of using this system, but ultimately, doing so will take some time.

Scanning Commands

Perhaps the most basic usage of Nmap is through scanning. When you want to scan, you have several different options. You can choose what you wish to target, whether it is one individual, several individuals, or an entire directory. Imagine for a moment that you want to scan a single unit or system. You would do so with the following command, changing the IP addresses accordingly.

nmap target
 # nmap target.com
 # nmap 192.143.1.1

This will scan that one specific system. If you wish to scan all associated subnets to that system, your command will change slightly. It would instead be:

nmap target/cdir
 # nmap 192.143.1.1/24

And if instead, you wanted to scan several different targets instead, you would simply label them and separate the IP addresses with spaces. For example, maybe you would write:

nmap target target1 target2
nmap 192.143.1.1 192.141.1.2

You even have the option to scan only several IP addresses in a row without scanning the entire subnet. When you wish to scan 50 of the associated IP addresses but not the entire subnet, you will use the following command:

nmap target-50
nmap 192.143.1.1-50

This would then lead to the scanning of every IP address from 192.143.1.1 to 192.143.1.50 all in one go.

You may also decide that what you need is a list of several hosts that are being scanned—in this case, you want to add the proper parameter. In this case, that parameter would be **-sL**, which would create the command prompt of:

nmap -sL target/cdir
nmap -sL 192.143.1.1/24

Sometimes, however, you may want to scan the entire subnet, but you also know that you need to leave a section of that subnet entirely unscanned in order to avoid detection.

Especially if you have the single IP address that you must avoid, you can then create your code with a parameter meant to exclude that one IP address. This is quite simple. All you need to do is add in the **-exclude¬** parameter like so:

---
nmap 192.143.1.1/24 - -exclude 192.143.1.13

You can even enter a single file that contains all excluded IP addresses if you have one, inserting the file name within the exclusion instead. Your scanning can even get more specific as well—you can start to specify exactly which ports are to be targeted if you have the right codes as well.

Scanning Techniques and Commands

Of course, there are other types of scans that you can perform as well. Nmap has several different scanning techniques available that will be necessary for you to know to be effective. This section will provide you with the information you will need to use several other scan types as well.

TCP SYN Scan

Commanded with the prompt **-sS** the TCP SYN scan is a basic scan. It is commonly referred to as half-opening because it gathers information from the remote host without finishing the TCP process that was discussed earlier in this book.

In this sort of scan, Nmap seeds out an SYN packet to the right destination but never bothers to actually create or trigger a session. In the end, the interaction never gets logged by the target computer because the computer never initiated a session. This is what makes TCP SYN scanning so beneficial. This is used by default, though you will need root access. Of course, if you are using Kali Linux as you do this, there will be no problem, as you will be in the root account by default. A command for this sort of scan looks like:

```
# nmap -sS 192.143.1.1
```

TCP Connect() Scan

When the SYN scan cannot happen for any reason, this will be the default scan that is used. With the code of **-sT** in order to utilize this scan, your system will instead complete the TCP handshake process, requiring the other system to log the transaction. This is only good for finding TCP ports rather than any others .To use this code, you would have a command such as:

```
# nmap -sT 192.143.1.1
```

UDP Scan

This scan seeks out open UDP ports in whatever the targeted machine is. It does not make use of an SYN packet due to the targeting of a UDP port instead. However, you are still able to make this more efficient if you use the –sS and **–sU** commands together.

In using this scanning method, Nmap sends out a UDP packet and waits for some sort of response. An error message implies that the port is closed, but a proper response will let you know that the port is actually open and accessible. In this case, you will use the following command:

---

nmap -sU 192.143.1.1

FIN Scan

Sometimes a TCP SYN scan would not necessarily be the right choice based on the parameters that you have been provided. Usually, a firewall will cause a block from the SYN packets, so you will need to go through another method. When this happens, you can try to make use of a FIN scan—this only sends a FIN flag, meaning it does not require the completion of the TCP transaction that would otherwise trigger the detection of Nmap. The proper command for a FIN scan is **–sF** such as:

---
nmap –sF 192.143.1.1

Which then brings back plenty of information—it should provide whether the host is up or down, what the latency is, and the state of the port. The target does not log this scan, but you are able to get the information.

Ping Scan

Unlike the other forms that have been discussed thus far, ping scanning is only used to determine if the host is currently alive or active. It does not discover whether a port is open. It does require root access, as there is the potential to send out ICMP packets. When there is no root access granted, it will complete the command using connect() call. The command for a ping scan is **-sP** and it would be used:

---
nmap -sP 192.143.1.1

Version Detection

This is the command you need if you want to determine what kind of software is being used on the target computer or any ports. It does not detect any open ports, though it does need to get the information from any open ports in order to provide the information on the software that has been detected.

The first step here would be to find a port that is open with a TCP SYN scan and then direct the **–sV** to the specific port available.

---
nmap –sV 192.143.1.1

Idle Scanning

In an idle scan, you are able to maintain your invisibility while scanning. In this particular technique, you do not send out any real packets from your own IP address. Instead, it takes a host from within the target network in order to send out packets. This will require you to first figure out an open port within the IP and then uses a zombie host in order to communicate with the target.

In this code, you will use first the IP of the zombie host and then the IP of the target in order to create a command of:

---
nmap -sl 192.143.1.4 192.143.1.1

In this instance, the zombie host of 192.143.1.4 is being used to communicate with 192.143.1.1 without detection since they are a part of the same network.

Penetration Testing

Ultimately, penetration testing can be broken down into seven steps or phases—when you are able to get through these phases, you are more likely to find some sort of weakness or vulnerability. In utilizing these phases, you will find that your own ability to break through a system grows. You will be more likely to crack through, which means that you are more likely to identify any of those weaknesses that you need to patch in your own system.

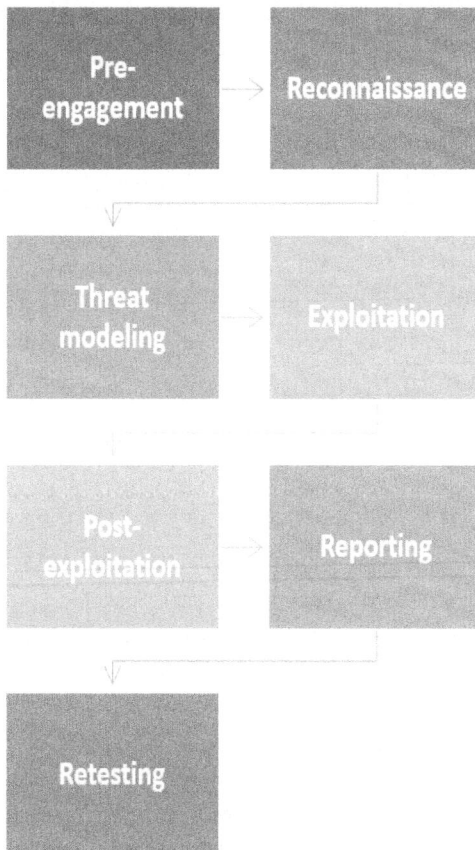

Pre-engagement	→	Reconnaissance
Threat modeling	→	Exploitation
Post-exploitation	→	Reporting
Retesting		

The phases of penetration testing are pre-engagement, reconnaissance, threat modeling, exploiting, post-exploit, report, and re-test. You will be guided through each of the steps during this section of this chapter.

Pre-Engagement

This particular step is more like a precaution, but it is crucial— when you are in the pre-engagement stage, you need to begin by figuring out the test's scope. Essentially, you are looking for the exact goals of your attempt to penetrate the network. You need to ensure that you know what you are planning out so you do not do anything unintended. Especially if you will be performing this as a possible career path, you need to get into the habit of laying out what you are going to do and what the limits on what you are and are not allowed to do are. You need to know exactly what is expected for you to do and which networks you should be focused on. Note it all down. If you are trying to crack into someone else's network at their behest, make sure you cover yourself legally and get signed documentation stating that you are working at their request and within their terms. Because penetration testing is dangerous by virtue of it attempting to chip away at security measures, you want to make sure that you are safe from being blamed if something were to go catastrophically wrong, which can occasionally happen.

Reconnaissance

At this stage, you are going to work on gathering information. While you may prefer to skip over this if you can get away with it, you are going to be more prepared if you actually know what you are doing. When you have the information that you need all lined up neatly in front of you, you will know what you expect.

In particular, you may want to gather information about the network you are targeting or the most likely types of technology you will be encountering. You may want to have personal information about the people that you are trying to hack into, or about their email addresses. When you are trying to sneak into a network, you never know what is and is not helpful or necessary. Gather as much information as you possibly can in order to be prepared and then move on to step 3, only after you are content that you have gathered anything that will be useful to you.

Threat Modeling and Identifying Vulnerabilities

Step 3 is still all about planning—at this point, you want to take all of the information that you have gathered in the previous steps and begin brainstorming up what the most realistic vulnerabilities and threats that the network would face would be. Does it use a certain network type that is particularly vulnerable to a specific plan of attack? Is there an exploit on the type of hardware they are using? Anything goes here, so long as it is a relevant threat that the target will likely face. This stage can also utilize a vulnerability scanner in order to scan the network for weaknesses. This could be done to find any vulnerabilities that are currently within that particular network, allowing you to calculate out the most likely vulnerabilities present. This can be a fantastic asset to you when you are trying to understand how best to access the network that you are attempting to penetrate. Kali Linux, luckily, comes with Metasploit—a way that you can scan for vulnerabilities within a list of specific target IPs. Metasploit will be discussed in-depth later within this book.

Another common technique at this stage is to use scanning tools and port scanners in order to find open ports or live hosts. In doing so, you may find that you are able to find another weakness that can be exploited to gain access. This technique allows you to scan devices, allowing for another point of entry. This is almost like reconnaissance v 2.0—here, you are making it a point to get more details about the systems. You should be able to identify what systems are present, whether or not they are currently up and active, or whether there are any sorts of firewalls or antivirus software installed. With your list of vulnerabilities identified, it is time to start figuring out more information as well. Can you get any valuable information form looking at the employees on the network? Is there value in finding customer data? Do customers have access to symptoms? Is there a possibility to steal financial information?

If there is, then it is quite possible that you may want to look somewhere other than surrounding the financial information first, in an effort to sneak around and figure out a better plan of attack rather than trying to run in, guns blazing, straight into a trap or an area that is heavily guarded. Think about the most likely possibilities in this situation and come up with a tentative plan of attack, but remember that your test is most likely going to be constantly evolving and changing as you get more and more information.

Exploitation

And now, it is time to begin attempting to access the network. You should have several different locations that you could use to attack the system and it is time to begin making those moves. Have you found any weaknesses that can be used to access? You may try to start a shell, or try to get some sort of credential assigned to you so you can begin to access as a root user instead.

Is there any room for using another computer's information to help you get head? The main part of this phase is attempting to gain as much access as you can without being detected and blocked out. While it is possible to do plenty of damage without ever actually gaining administrative accesses and permissions, most of the time, what you are attempting to do is get that permission. This stage will be largely dependent upon the network that you are attempting to break through, and you will need to be creative. Make sure that you document what does and does not work as you go so you can start to figure things out. Remember, if you are doing this for yourself or for a client, you are going to want to know exactly what worked and what did not. When you have gotten as much information as you can here, it is time for the next stage.

Post-Exploitation

Next comes the post-exploitation phase. At this point, you will have finished testing, either due to running out of tie or having reached the end of your ability to exploit or run out of the system to exploit. At this point, you must make a list of all vulnerabilities and provide them to the client. As you have gone through, you should have made notes, or potentially screenshots, of anything that did or did not work. You should be able to figure out how significant the exploit that you have done is—did you get into the main server or did you get stuck at a computer with little sophisticated access to the server? How valuable was the information that you got from the system, if any? How at risk is the system itself?

Beyond that, you should also be thinking of how to fix any vulnerabilities that were discovered. Can you think of an easy patch to solve the problem? Is there something else that you can do to ensure that the network is more secure? What can the network do better? What worked well? Beyond that, you should also make sure that you clean up as well.

You need to remove anything that was planted within the system and change back any and all settings to what they used to be. You want to make sure that everything that you have exploited is removed.

Reporting

At this stage, it is time to come up with your report. It may not be fun, but if you have gone through the penetration testing in order to help someone, you need to make sure that your report is written up nice and neatly. This is where you are able to convey any weaknesses and vulnerabilities that will put the client at risk.

You will make sure that you are able to tell them which exploits happened and how they should be fixed.

This stage should be as brutally honest as possible—you want the other party to know exactly what happened and how to fix it. If their system is truly that vulnerable to exploitation and you were able to get access to everything, let it loose. Tell them in unbiased but honest terms exactly how things went wrong. This is where they are also given an example plan of action to make sure that everything gets patched up. The clearer you make this stage for the client, the better you will be at your job and the more likely it will be that your client is able to fix the problems and secure the network.

Retesting

This is not a stage that everyone is willing to go through as penetration testers, but it is an important one if you want to do a thorough job in doing so. During this stage, you will give the client time to look through their own vulnerabilities and attempt to repair them and you reevaluate their attempts to bolster their defenses. You will essentially retest the parts that were fixed in order to see that they actually did patch up any vulnerability that was there. You may not always be asked to do this, but if you are, it is always an act of good faith to go through with it.

CHAPTER 6
How to Become and Remain Anonymous

Anonymity is crucial if you hope to be a hacker, no matter the kind. If you are not careful, it becomes incredibly easy to simply blacklist your specific IP address and you no longer have that access. Instead of managing to get through the system or finding any exploits, you instead end up banned and unable to do anything. However, that does not have to be your fate if you are trying to hack—you can instead cover your tracks. Just as many burglars will wear gloves in order to hide their fingerprints from the system that they are trying to access, making sure that you put on your own metaphorical digital gloves can help you remain anonymous. This means that your information will be private—you will be able to disguise yourself and your software in order to make sure that your real IP address is not being used.

Now, you may be thinking, what if you are using a virtual machine? Would that not have a digitized IP address or be hidden more because the entire thing is digital? Yes and no— however, that is still only as secure as the network that you are using. This means that if you really want true anonymity, you are going to want to involve the usage of something else as well. You are going to want to add in extra tools and precautions to arm yourself against your IP address is found out. When you are able to fight it off, you are more likely to remain anonymous.

There are several tools out there that would be able to aid you with the process of being anonymous and protecting yourself, all built within Kali Linux and ready to be used. All it will take is the time and effort to configure everything, but it will be well worth the effort. The three methods in particular that will be discussed within this chapter will be proxy servers, VPNs, and the use of TOR. Within each section, you will be guided through what the particular method is, how it works, and how to use it with Kali Linux.

Proxy

- Obscuring the IP address through disguising them

VPN

- Creating an extra layer between your own personal IP address and the internet for security

Tor

- Having your digital footprint constantly shifted from place to place around the world to hide your trail

Proxychains

Perhaps one of the simplest methods to obscure your IP address is through the use of a proxy server. Through using chains of proxies, you are able to obscure your tracks, making them harder to follow. In making them more difficult to follow, you will be more likely to avoid detection. When you use a proxy, of course that proxy is logging your information. However, you can get around this as well—you can string together several proxies together in a chain. So long as at least one proxy is able to be outside of the jurisdiction of the target, you should be able to avoid the problem altogether.

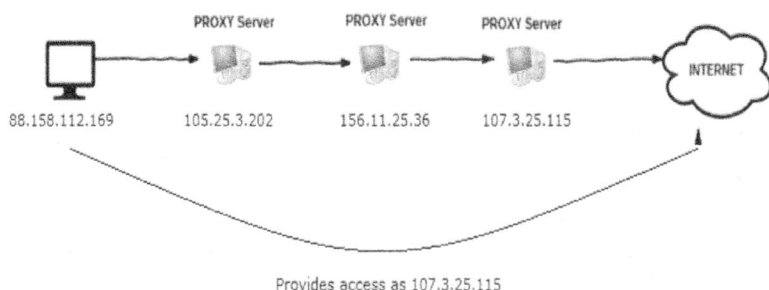

Provides access as 107.3.25.115

Luckily, within Kali, you have access to a tool known as Proxychains. This can be found within your directory, which you can pull up with a location command. It will most likely be in the /usr/bin directory. When you are using Proxychains, you will be using a very straightforward command:

> # proxychains [enter command that is proxied] [add in any arguments]

Now, imagine that you wanted to use this with Nmap to scan anonymously and through a proxy. Perhaps in particular, you want to use a TCP SYN scan on the IP address 192.143.1.1 but you want to do so through a proxy utilizing the tool. In this case, you would create a command prompt of:

> # proxychains nmap -sS 192.143.1.1

This then triggers you to do the TCP SYN scan on that one particular IP address through a proxy.

With the syntax understood, you are able to move on to completing a config file. As with basically anything else within Linux, there are simple text files known as config files that will hold all of the necessary information. You are able to open these in any of the text editors you have, such as via gedit or leafpad. Open the config file into your text editor and you should see a file with all sorts of information. Within it, you will find that one particular area has a spot for you to add the proxy. You will simply enter the IP address of any proxies that you are utilizing there.

Typically, proxychains will default to Tor, as you can see within your file. If you will be using Tor, leave this as is. If you are not using Tor, you will need to make the appropriate edits to the file. This book will be moving forward with Tor.

With the proxy server set up, it is time to test it. You can do so by sending out a scan through the proxy. When you send the scan out, you should see your chosen IP address listed and it should line up with your proxy one. Beyond just setting up the proxy, however, you can do plenty of other things with this as well. You can add several proxies, for example, and then chain them together so they chain either at random, in a specific order, or uses only part of them.

Start by opening your proxychains config file again. You will then look at the dynamic_chains line—you can see that it is commented out. This means that it will not be used at this moment. If you erase the comment mark, it should activate when the process is run.

You can also find random chaining as well within your file. You can re-add the # to comment out the dynamic_chains line and instead remove the # from the random_chain option instead. You can only make use of one or the other of these options at any given time, so you will have to go back in and remove one if you wish to use the other.

VPN

Another layer of security that you can add to your system is through adding a VPN on top of the use of proxy addresses. This is common practice—it allows for further protection from piracy or other issues. It also allows people to bypass, for example, any particular activities that may be illegal within a country. It also can allow you to scan other networks without being detected—something else that is commonly considered to be illegal in several countries. Even just scanning the network can be enough to lead to it being considered illegal, even though you may not have done anything with it. Now, since you are currently reading about how best to do exactly that, you are going to find that the extra security is crucial to protecting yourself.

VPN Software
(Secures your data)

YOU

INTERNET

There are several reasons to use a VPN, all of which are incredibly compelling. Not only does a VPN allow you to cloak your IP address and therefore protect you, but it also allows you to use any network while ensuring that there is still encryption.

Further, you will be able to log into your sensitive information without worrying about it being hijacked if you are on another network. You will be able to skip past any monitoring that may have been installed, or access region-restricted websites.

Of course, it is also important to recognize that your VPN will not cloak everything—there will be some ways to identify you. For example, your regular search engine can probably recognize you simply due to cookies and browsing behavior, especially if you are already logged into an account with that particular engine. Despite the shortcomings, however, the fact that a VPN can help you hide more means that you can rely on it to provide you with more protection than you would otherwise have. Just as a seatbelt is not a guarantee of safety in a car accident, a VPN is not a guarantee of security—however it is an extra layer that is there to help keep you safe if necessary. When you want to enable a VPN on Kali Linux, you will have a handful of commands to use and steps to follow, but in the end, you will add extra protection to your software, meaning that you will be able to better protect yourself.

Step 1: Enable VPN

The VPN option is usually disabled by default when you use Kali Linux, so you will have to open it up before continuing. This will require you to enter your own command, such as:

 # apt-get install network-manager-openvpn

This particular command is specific to enable a VPN. At this point, you may need to restart your networking and network-manager. Upon the restart, you should find that the VPN is now available.

Step 2: Download and Extract OpenVPN

Now, you will need to download the openvpn.zip file. This is not particularly difficult—a code such as:

 # wget https://www.privateinternetacess.com/openvpn/ openvpn.zip

To download the file. Once it is downloaded and saved, you will then need to unzip the file and make sure it is deposited into the right directory for later use. You can do this with the following command:

```
# unzip -q openvpn.zip –d /etc/openvpn
```

Your file should be ready, and now it is time to move on to step 3.

Step 3: Configure Network Manager to use PIA VPN

At this step, you will be setting up Network Manager so it will recognize and allow the use of the VPN that you are hoping to set up. This will involve you going into Network Manager, editing the connections, then swapping to the VPN tab and selecting that you would like to add it. You would then click on ADD, at which point, you would then set the type as OpenVPN. Then, click on create.

If you go to VPN, you will find several important details that will allow you to tell whether or not you are actually using the proper VPN in the first place. In this case, you should see a connection name of PrivateInternetAccess VPN, a gateway that should be closest to your own personal location, a username that you can set in, a password that you can save, and then the CA certificate.

To get the CA certificate, you must go to /etc/openvpn in order to access the right directory, and then select on ca.crt to use it within this stage.

Now, click on **Advanced** and choose the box that is next to **Use LZO data compression**. You then must click on **OK**, then save and close the window.

At this point, if you click on Network Manager > VPN Connections > PrivateInternetAccess VPN, you should see a yellow connection indicator. Your VPN is now ready for use.

Tor and Kali Linux

Tor is yet another layer in the security umbrella that you can create in order to ensure that you are able to protect yourself. This is just another security precaution, but if you make good use of it, you can find that you are actually able to really protect yourself, especially if you begin to layer these safety methods together to protect your anonymity as much as possible. Remember, Kali Linux is already secure, but you are able to add extra layers to it utilizing the tools within its repository. Tor is another of those particular tools that are able to help protect you that comes with the Kali Linux toolset.

Tor itself is free software and will protect you through actively bouncing your communication throughout several different network points. Essentially, there is a massive network created by volunteers around the world. They help transfer your information erratically so it cannot really be tracked easily. In constantly bouncing your information from place to place, you essentially end up with your data being highly protected. Your history will not be easily tracked and the sites that you are visiting are not able to know exactly where you are physical.

Effectively, you block yourself from being seen because people all over the world send your signals and information all over the place. One request may originate in the United States while another pops up in Spain and another in Germany. Especially if you layer this with the previously discussed methods for real anonymity, you become incredibly difficult to track. You would not only have a series of different IP addresses being cycled through, but you would also have those IP addresses encrypted and protected by your VPN, and then you would further have protection because your access to the internet is being passed through Tor instead of through your usual methods.

When you want to use Tor on your Kali Linux machine, you will have to install it manually. Because you are on Kali, you are locked into being the root user, which means that you cannot use the shortcut mode that you are usually able to utilize. Instead of being able to utilize any shortcuts, you will need to manually download the Tor download.

You can do this through the Tor Project official website. You will want to get the bundle download from their website and then download the torbrowser-launcher from GitHub.

Make sure that you download the architecture appropriate files and save it somewhere that you are able to access. Then, utilizing the tar command, you should extract the package from the download directory. You can do this with the following command:

 # tar –xvf tor

Keep in mind that this command believes that the only file within your directory that begins with "tor" is your file for the tore download.

Then, you need to run the Tor Browser Bundle. This will require you using the start-tor-browser script that you have just extracted:

 # ./start-tor-browser.desktop

In doing so, you will see Vidalia launched, and that will connect to Tor. With Tor connected to, Firefox will launch.

If you are able to utilize these three different methods for privacy in tandem, you may quickly find that you are actually able to protect yourself greatly from the risks out in the real world of the internet. You will be able to ensure that your IP address is not as likely to be discovered, especially if you are messing around with some of the particular interests of those using Kali Linux, such as penetration testing that may otherwise become problematic.

CHAPTER 7
Metasploit Framework

Penetration testing is something that has already been discussed within this book, but it will be mentioned again. Within Kali Linux, you are granted access to all sorts of fantastic tools that can help you with your process of hacking, penetration testing, and searching for vulnerabilities or access points. One such tool for penetration testing that has not been discussed yet is a tool known as the Metasploit Framework. This particular tool utilizes Command line alterations or GUI. It can also be used as a sort of support method that can be used for all sorts of purposes. This tool is incredibly powerful and is used by both cybercriminals and ethical hackers alike due to the usefulness of the program. In particular, Metasploit allows for the probing of any systematic vulnerabilities within a network or server, and is also open-source, meaning that the framework can be easily modified to work for anyone and with nearly any operating system.

What is Metasploit?

In particular, Metasploit refers to a specific tool that is used. The pen testing team that is using it will be able to use either code that was already made for them or custom code that they have created and then inject it into a network. In doing so, the flaws within that particular network become discovered and are brought to attention.

This means then that they are able to address the weaknesses of that particular network so they can be addressed. Really, then, Metasploit is just another exploitative tool, much like Nmap, though it serves a different purpose. However, it is important to recognize that the tool itself is not evil or unethical. The tool itself is designed to be used for ethical hackers.

The Metasploit Project came about in 2003 to use as a Perl-based portable network tool. However, by 2007, it was converted to Ruby and instead was licensed by Rapid7, where it has remained. Some of the tools within the Metasploit framework, which is larger than Metasploit itself, include several other tools that are regularly used within Kali Linux. These tools all have different purposes and the Metasploit framework as becoming one of the default choices in development and mitigation. Before this, probes used to have to be performed manually, making pen testing incredibly slow-going, exhausting, and tedious.

The framework has even grown to include some proprietary tools rather than the free offerings that have been built into Kali Linux. These tools, such as Metasploit Pro and Metasploit Express offer their own benefits, however, they are unnecessary if you do not want to use them.

Metasploit Users

Thanks to how wide the range of applications for Metasploit, it is used from ethical hackers that wish to make their own operating systems and servers more protected to those who are legitimately interested in breaking into an OS for nefarious purposes. It is, however, an incredibly reliable tool that is easy to install and useful.

No matter the language that you choose to use or which platform you are utilizing, Metasploit should work, and this is a pretty significant part of why Metasploit is so incredibly popular in the first place. It is so useful in making sure that it is readily accessible that it has become widespread.

As of now, Metasploit includes over 1600 exploits for 25 different platforms, and it carries nearly 500 payloads. This all comes together to create such a powerful tool that people cannot help but enjoy it.

Some of the payloads that are included are:

- **Command shell payloads**: They enable people to run scripts or commands against a different target or host

- **Dynamic payloads**: They allow testers to come up with unique payloads as they attempt to avoid any antivirus software

- **Meterpreter payloads:** They allow for the overtaking of device monitors to overtake other sessions

- **Static payloads**: They enable ports to be forwarded and communications to be had between networks.

Metasploit Users

There are several modules included within Metasploit. These are core components—software that have very specific actions that they are supposed to perform. These also represent the actions that you can achieve within the Metasploit framework. These modules are readily located: all you have to do is find the following repository:

/path/to/metasploit/apps/pro/msf3/modules

The module type will be determined by the purpose of that particular one, as well as the action that the particular module is responsible for. In particular there are eight that are worthy of discussing.

These include:

Exploits:

Exploit modules are designed to execute a series of commands that then target a vulnerability that has been discovered within the targeted system or application. This module is designed to take advantage of any vulnerability in order to provide access to whatever the target system is. There are several different examples of exploit modules, such as code injection and web application exploits.

Payloads:

A payload refers to a shell code that runs after the exploit has managed to compromise the system at hand. The payload allows you to decide exactly how you want to be able to connect to the shell and what it is that you want to be done to the target after you have taken control of it. It can involve opening a meterpreter or a different command shell. The Meterpreter is specifically an advanced type of payload that allows for the writing of DLL files, allowing for new features as you need them to be created.

Encoders:

The encoders are critical tools that are able to convert one form of code into another.

Listeners:

Malware that is designed to hide to listen. When they are able to listen, they are able to gather up all sorts of important information, allowing for sensitive information, such as passwords, social security numbers, or other information that people would largely like to keep private to be leaked.

Auxiliary Function:

Tools and commands meant to supplement the other functions of the device

Shellcode:

Code programmed to activate as soon as it is inside the target in order to do specific purposes, allowing for a more discrete way to get in and activate.

NOP generator:

This is a tool that is able to produce a series of random bytes that are designed to bypass any standard IDs in order to get past firewalls or important blockages.

Post-exploitation code:

The post-exploitation modules allow you to get more information or manage to steal further access within an exploited target. These include hash dumps or service enumerators.

Using Metasploit

When you have Metasploit installed and ready to use, all you need to do is gather information somehow, whether through first port scanning or finding a vulnerability scanner to find a way in.

Once you are in, all you have to do is choose an exploit and payload and Metasploit will do the rest for you. Effectively, the exploit is the way that weakness is identified and in harder to defend networks.

The framework is specifically designed to make use of various models and interfaces, such as msfconsole interactive curses, and more. It can work from the terminal/cmd, and is also compatible with the Metasploit Community Web Interface, which will support pen testing.

Installing Metasploit

Before you can use Metasploit, however, you must first install it. Installing it will require you to first disable all of your firewalls and antivirus software. Due to the file itself, it is oftentimes considered malicious when you try to install it with your firewalls and antivirus software running. This then interrupts your installation. Because of this, it is best to just disable the firewall and antivirus software first before continuing. This means as well, however, that you must also make sure that you are ensuring that your source of download is legitimate and safe. If you are not careful, you may inadvertently download something that actually could be dangerous or problematic to you.

With the firewalls and antivirus software down, make sure that you also have your administrative privileges. This should not be a problem in Kali Linux as you should already have root user access by default, but if you are not for some reason or you are attempting to install Metasploit on a different distro of Linux, you are going to want to ensure that you also have that administrator privilege for yourself.

Finally, to install Metasploit, your best bet is to install it from the Rapid7 site. Doing so will allow you to get the installer for your specific operating system. It also will contain a self-contained environment that you can use for updating and running the framework. This means that everything that you need will all be taken care of during the initial installation process. You can, of course, go in manually to configure Metasploit yourself if you choose to do so, but that step is unnecessary and will be skipped for the purpose of this book. When you have the files, launch the installer. It will prompt you to enter a specific framework. As a Kali Linux user, you should find that this is preinstalled and not have to continue further.

Managing the Metasploit Database

Now, it is time to stop and finish the database information before continuing. When you are ready to manage your database, you will need to use the msfdb script to configure postgresql to run in order to store the database in ~/.msf4/db/

When ready to start this, you will use the following command:

$ msfdb init

This will trigger the database to start, and you will then be able to use any of several commands that will work best for you. These commands add extra functionality and help you manage the space that you have available. The most common commands at this stage that you will need to include

msfdb reinit - This will cause your database to be deleted and reinitialized in order to refresh it.

msfdb delete - Using this particular command will lead to your database being deleted altogether without it reinitializing as the previous command caused.

msfdb start - This command starts the database back up again, allowing it to begin running

msfdb stop - This command, when used, will stop the database from running at all

msfdb status - This command will allow the terminal to print the current database status, showing you all of the critical information within the terminal.

The Metasploit Datastore

Beyond just having everything that has been listed thus far, there is also the datastore—another core component of the Metasploit framework that is often overlooked altogether. This is a series of values that will allow you to configure any behaviors that you desire within the Metasploit framework. The datastore allows interfaces to change settings, while the payloads are able to patch up opcodes, and exploits are able to specify specific parameters. This also allows for the framework to pass between modules as well.

In particular, Metasploit has two different datastores: the global and module datastore. You will need to be familiar with both in order to use Metasploit effectively. The global datastore can allow for all modules to use it. When the datastore option is set, all modules will have access to it. In order to define the global datastore option, you will need to use the command: **setg**

The module datastore, on the other hand, is designed so only designated modules will be able to utilize it, rather than anyone at all.

The Metasploit Workspaces

The workspaces within Metasploit allow you to segment up the hosts and data within the database. This allows you to use the workspaces to create separations between any of the segments that you wish to test.

For example, imagine that you want a workspace for every single subnet within your organization because you want to limit the number of hosts to a specified network. This would lead to you creating workspaces such as one per department. This means that each organization's department would get its own workspaces.

When you use a workspace, you are able to import data, manipulate that data, and then export that data right back out in order to ensure that the data can be reused automatically. This also allows for the same workspace to automatically report anything about any current host that is being engaged with. This allows for information such as vulnerabilities to be transmitted.

If you wish to create a workspace, you must use the workspace command with the –a option in order to do so. Whatever workspace you create becomes the current one being used.

Imagine for a moment that you want one for the three departments, A, B, and C in your organization.

You would write:

- **msf workspace –a A**

- **msf workspace –a B**

- **ms workspace –a C**

Overall, of course, if you are ready to use Metasploit, you should find that it is actually incredibly easy to get involved with. All you will need to know is how to go through the system and how to understand what you are looking at. When you know which kinds of modules are available, for example, you will be able to choose those that work for you.

Because Metasploit is already jam-packed with all sorts of information for you that is designed to ensure that you are able to do almost anything with just a few commands instead of having to constantly manually be telling your system what you want it to do, it is actually incredibly user-friendly. This is exactly why it has become so popular.

Ultimately, you should be just fine with the free version that comes with Linux, though there are upgrades available if you care to pay for them, and ultimately, that will be a personal opinion and you will have to decide based on your own thoughts and desires. Of course, the upgraded versions, even though they boast quite the hefty price tags, are designed to be incredibly powerful for you. They are aimed at highly skilled pen tester professionals who know exactly what they are doing and exactly what they are getting, and they are able to justify that massive price tag. However, you do not have to do this as well.

CHAPTER 8
Digital Certificate

Just as how in the real world, we need to carry identification to prove who we are, especially when we are doing something major, such as buying a car or taking out a loan, your internet connection also needs some level of identification as well. This is where digital certificates come in. When you have servers full of valuable information, you likely want to ensure that your information is as protected as possible at all times—this makes sense. However, how are you supposed to be certain that those who are accessing the information on your server are truly who they said they were or truly allowed to be accessing it?

Especially in this day and age, when we are so concerned with data being stolen or taken over, it is easy to feel like our data is at risk, and for a good reason—it is. When you introduce a layer of digital certificates, however, you add an extra layer of safety to your servers or to feel like your private information is protected.

You are able to make sure that, though you are using sites that may be on the public internet, your data itself is certified.

If you have a LAN, however, you may not need this sort of major certification that would come along with using the public network for data. The cost of paying for those certificates may be unnecessary compared to the risk.

In those instances, the best idea to secure a network is to use your own local CA or certificate authority—this will automatically sign any certificates that are actively installed within your LAN in order to protect their servers. Most often, this is done with a tool known as OpenSSL—something that comes prepackaged with Kali Linux. We will be discussing how to create a certificate shortly, but for now, we will return our focus to the background information first.

This chapter will first discuss what a digital certificate and the certificate authorities that exist. From there, you will be walked through how to create a digital certificate on your Kali Linux based web servers. Being able to create your own digital certificate definitely has its own uses, but comes with its own issues as well. Nevertheless, if you think that it may be useful to you, you are more than welcome to pursue it. At the very least, it is more command language under your belt that you can use. At best, you may find some legitimate use in it.

What is a Digital Certificate?

The digital certificate is essentially the way to link the ownership of a public key on the internet to the individual that owns it. These are used for sharing public keys for encrypting and authenticating data. When you use these, you effectively end up with a way to safeguard the digital signature.

Within a digital certificate, there are several layers of information that all serve different purposes—there is the public key that is certified. There is information that is identifying whoever is the owner of a said public key. There is metadata that is directly related to the digital certificate, and there is a digital signature of that particular public key, generated by the certificate issuer.

Effectively, the public key comes in a pair—there is the public key that is used to lock the data that needs to be authenticated, and there is the private key that is held by the owner, used to sign and decrypt the protected data. Effectively, this leads to the digital certificate owner sharing the public key with their data that has been encrypted so they are able to access it with the private key that goes along with it.

These days most major web browsers utilize digital certificates—this allows people to know that the content that they are viewing has not been altered by someone who did not have permission to do so, and allows decrypting and encrypting of web content. Effectively, this is just another way to develop the privacy and protection that people are looking for in their interactions with the internet. While you are able to issue your own PKI (public key infrastructure) and we will discuss doing that shortly, for the most part, there is some sort of organization that usually manages the creation and distribution of PKIs. This organization is known as the certificate authority.

Certificate Authorities

The certificate authority is a trusted third party who maintains the PKI, issuing out digital certificates and protecting them from being attacked or exploited in any way. By using a third party to authenticate a website and ensure that it is protected, websites are able to prove that they are actually safer than people may otherwise think. They are able to prove that they are legitimately interested and concerned in maintaining the safety of the customers and other people who are actively accessing their site because they are actively paying for that extra level of security. The individuals feel like their data is better protected, which leads to a higher likelihood of people returning to that particular site again. They are willing to take the shot if they feel like they can trust the source.

Types of Certificates

Ultimately, there are several types of certificates that can be provided for an individual. These certificates either come from a different source or with a different purpose and they will be treated differently depending on the type of certificate that it is. The various certificates that can be used will be discussed in this section. The certificates exist in a sort of chain with each other, with one validating the other.

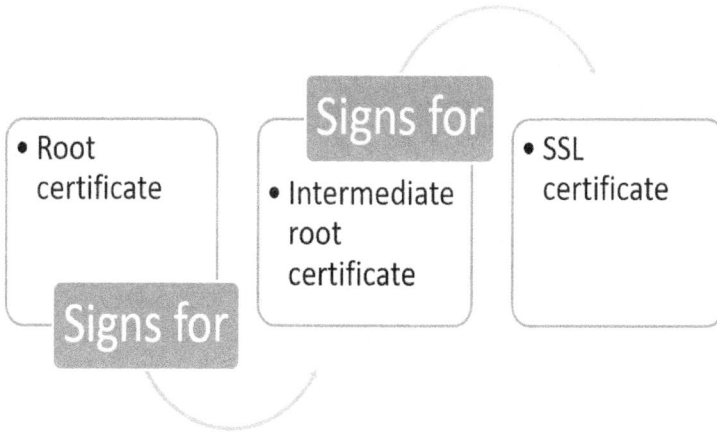

- Root certificate

Signs for

- Intermediate root certificate

- SSL certificate

Signs for

Root Certificate

The root certificate is a public key certificate that is meant to identify a root certificate authority (Root CA). Anyone is capable of generating a signing key and signing that new certificate, though it is not considered to be valid until it is signed by the trusted or valid CA.

The root certificate is the top of the chain, essentially—it must be given by a trusted certificate. These are typically related to the software that you are using—if you are using Microsoft, for example, it is likely that your root certificate is signed by Microsoft.

Effectively, each of the certificate programs has its own sort of guidelines and stores of root certificates that can be used. These have the toughest standards for one reason—if you have one of these certificates, you are seen to be trusted. The root certificate is necessary in order to make sure that other certificates are issued and verified.

Intermediate Certificate

The intermediate certificate is the one in the middle—certificate authorities do not tend to directly issue their own certificates. Because of this, they instead use what is known as an intermediate root. This certificate is used by the CA to sign in and allow them to issue any end user SSL certificates. In doing this, there can be several intermediate root stops before you eventually arrive at the SSL certificate. Eventually, however, you reach the end user, who gets the SSL.

SSL Certificate

The final certificate, the end result, is the secure sockets layer—this is the global standard technology that allows for the use of encrypted communication between a browser and a server. These are used by millions of people and businesses everywhere to protect data from hackers or identity thieves. Effectively, the SSL allows for the conversation between the user and the server to be kept private, even though it is happening on the public web network.

These are typically issued by a certificate authority, who is trusted to ensure that the data will, in fact, be protected as promised. The SSL layer comes in several different types of certificates—they can be domain validated, organization validated, or extended validation.

Domain validated SSL certificates tell the least and promise the least—all you need to do to get this SSL is prove that you are using the right domain name. This does show that the data is being sent and received as intended to the one who holds the certificate, there is no way to prove who that certificate holder is. Organization validated SSL certificates provide slightly more assurance—they confirm that the holder does have some sort of right or claim to use a specific domain but also undergo extra confirmation to ensure that the individual with the certificate does, in fact, own the domain.

The extended validation certificate, on the other hand, is issued after applicants are able to prove that they are who they say they are to the standards of whatever CA is vetting them.

This process requires the verification of the existence of the individual or entity who wishes to apply for the certificate, while also guaranteeing that the identity matches any official records as well. Effectively, the entity is verified and authorized to use that domain and certificate.

Generating Self-Signed SSL Certificates

As you are likely to expect, Kali Linux comes with its own program that allows it to create certificates. This is done through OpenSSL. While this will not always work for you and may, in fact, get rejected when you attempt to use it, you are able to do so. You are able to provide all of the encryption benefits with your self-signed SSL certificate, but you will not get the authentication benefits. This means that not many people will be able to trust your site, and it is likely that anyone who tries to access your site will get a warning that says that your site or server is not, in fact, verified and therefore cannot be guaranteed.

Despite that, it can be useful to have, even if just for yourself. This section will discuss the steps necessary to create your own SSL certificates.

First, open up OpenSSL. There, you must use the following commands:

---

openssl genrsa –out key.pem 2048
openssl req –new –sha256 –key key.pem –out csr.csr
oepnssl req –x509 –sha256 –days 365 –key key.pem –in csr.csr –out certificate.pem

---

The first command triggers a 2048-bit RSA private key—this is the recommended format for your key to be in and it will be generated at that first command.

The second command triggers the creation of a certificate signing request—you will likely get questions at that second command and it is your job to answer them as accurately as possible to guarantee that you are seen as trustworthy.

The third command triggers the generation of a self-signed x509 certificate that is usable on web servers. This is exactly what you were looking for.

Remember, these will encrypt the site and make sure that your data is protected, but it does not actually offer authentication benefits.

They can obviously still have their uses, such as when protecting a site during early stages, but due to the warning, you are not likely to want to keep this as your only form of verification if you will be expecting long-term traffic or you will be handling any sort of sensitive information such as payment methods or addresses.

Ultimately, you will need to figure out just how worthwhile paying for a legitimate certificate may be if you do not want to deal with security warnings chasing people away.

CHAPTER 9
Bash and Python Scripting

B ash itself is a shell—it stands for Bourne Again SHell, and it serves an important purpose. It allows for starting the server, confirming that the server is open, and working to keep everything running smoothly. Effectively, the shell on a system is meant to take any commands that you input through your keyboard in order to tell the operating system what to do. This was the only real way to interact with your Unix-like system back in the day, but these days, we have access to so much more. You are able to use GUIs alongside CLIs these days, meaning that you no longer have to type out what you want your computer to do if you want it to do so. This is why instead of typing out where your file is in order to locate it, you can simply go to your start menu, click, search through the files manually, and then open it up.

There is no denying that bash has a history—it is what was effectively initially used by those who were accessing their original systems, and while it was absolutely useful then, there is question now about whether it is still the best way to be interacting. It is like the stubborn old coworker that has been at her job forever and refuses to change, despite the fact that her way is clunky, inefficient, and really, redundant. Everyone would be happier if she went to the easier version, and productivity and ease of the work would go up, but she refuses.

This same sort of resistance appears with bash and transitioning from bash to another language, such as Python, which is currently one of the top contenders as a replacement.

The idea these days is that the shell may be becoming obsolete— there are better ways to interact with your operating system. In particular, the shell has several concerning features:

- The syntax is obscure sometimes

- It is slow

- It is easy to accidentally leave out something crucial

- The shell's language's data structure is a string

- It is difficult to test units on the shell

Each of these lends their hands toward the idea of replacing the shell. While the shell has been used as a legitimate programming language, it is incomplete—it is not designed to be a complete programming language, but Python is.

Python itself is an interpreted, high-level programing language that is meant to be dynamic. It is meant to be object-oriented, it is meant to be layered. It is meant to be used as either a scripting language or even as a sort of binding agent between two different applications or components.

Python is quite simple to learn and is focused on providing an easily readable system, allowing for it to be easier to access than some more complex languages that may emphasize old, outdated phrases or syntaxes that are simply used out of tradition and familiarity at this point. However, familiarity is not always a good thing.

Sometimes, what is needed more than ever is a change, or at least to adapt in some way in order to ensure that you are able to keep growing. This is where Python and bash meet.

Effectively, then, the best way to up productivity would be from moving away from the use of the shell and instead, work with Python code instead. Because Python is easier to read, is faster, and allows for legitimate testing, it seems like shifting over to it, at least in some capacity would be beneficial.

Interestingly enough, Python is already installed by default on major Linux distributions. If you were to open a command prompt and type in "python" you should be provided with a Python interpreter. This alone suggests that it may be worth the use of Python over bash when considering the creation of scripting. Thanks to the ease of use alone, it would save time.

Take a look at some of the most compelling reasons to shift from focusing on shell scripts to using Python as a replacement instead:

- **It is installed by default**

- **It is easy to read and the syntax is simple**

- **It is an interpreted language**

- **It is a fully-featured programming language**

- **Python has access to a standard library and plenty of third-party libraries in order to use all sorts of utilities**

- **Python's standard library is sorted by date and time, allowing you to put a date into any format to compare it to other dates**

- **Python is a simpler transitional link**

The assertion here is not to step away from the shell altogether—the shell absolutely has its own purposes. However, the shell also is weak in several aspects. Think about how much nicer it would be to navigate through several of your tasks in a much simpler manner—it would be nice to have syntax and commands that make more sense rather than being remembered simply because of you now that you were supposed to remember them.

Of course, there are areas where bash is, undoubtedly simpler. This is exactly why the two should be brought together.

When they are drawn together, they are able to bring out the best in each other—you will have the best of both worlds thanks to having a system that is capable of transitioning between the two with ease. Python is more complete and more readily used in several different contexts whereas bash was designed with Linux in mind.

It is impossible to deny that some of bash is just nicer to use. For example, consider moving a file from your desktop to a directory on bash:

 # cd Desktop# mv folder directory

Notice how nice and neat that is. Now, in Python, it would look more like:

Import os globfor fname in glob.glob ('folder):os.rename (fname, 'directory')

There is no denying that the Python code is unnecessarily bulky, especially when standing next to that short and sweet blurb from bash.

This is exactly why it would be best to utilize the two together rather than trying to disentangle them and replacing one or the other.

While we have already discussed that it is possible for you to bring in your Python code within your shell, it is also possible to go the other direction as well—you can introduce your Python script within your shell and you can insert your shell scripts within Python as well. All you need to do is import the OS module. If you do so, you will be able to make use of your bash commands within Python as well—this means that you are effectively able to mix and match your commands with ease.

Think of how children who have grown up speaking two languages at home tend to seamlessly shift from one to the next within the same sentence, inserting a few words in one language while also inserting some of the other languages interchangeably, creating what sounds like something that would be impossible to understand, but they do so with ease. This is what you would be doing with Python by inserting bash as well.

In order to bring bash language to python, all you have to do is:

$ python >>>from os import *>>> system ('sudo apt-get update')

And you should now have access to both languages.

You should absolutely try to tinker around with both languages. If you are not familiar with Python yet, you may feel inclined to go through the effort of learning it—it is incredibly simple to pick up and if you were already able to pick up communicating with Linux, you should be able to pick up understanding Python as well.

All you have to do is put in some of the efforts that once went to developing your skills with Linux toward learning this system as well. You will likely find that with the increased productivity, you will quickly grow fond of the change.

If you are unsure whether you have Python currently installed on your system, you are in luck—finding out, you will need to enter the following command:

$ python –version

You will most likely get an older and stable form of Python that is sufficient, but you will likely want to upgrade that form into the more recent version. This version is constantly changing, so it is for the best if you go check the version that is available to you upon reading this book—you can do this by simply searching for the most recent version online and then updating.

If you do decide to pursue Python in particular, you will want to go and find some guides and books, not unlike this one that you are reading right now to find out what you need to know. Tutorials and web lessons are always fantastic starting stones for you to begin experimenting with Python. Eventually, as you become more comfortable and familiar, you may decide to begin intertwining your attempts to use both languages together. You may even decide that you prefer Python over using the shell, and that is fine too. Ultimately, technology is changing so rapidly that you cannot afford to hold yourself back with a fear of changing or growing or shifting to something new—transitioning and learning are absolutely beneficial to you.

Now, as this chapter and this book come to a close, it is time for you to begin thinking about how to put everything together. It is time to consider whether you are really interested in Kali Linux at all or if you would prefer to learn something else. What is for sure, however, is that ultimately, you must guide yourself and your own decisions in order to ensure that you are happy with what you have chosen to do.

CONCLUSION

Congratulations—you have made it to the end of Kali Linux Hacking. This book is designed to be a crash course in learning Kali Linux—the operating system designed specifically for penetration testing by penetration testing professionals for the use of finding and repairing any sorts of weaknesses or exploits that are found within the system. If you have made it this far, you must have been quite interested in either installing Kali Linux, or you have used this book as a guide, and regardless of which of those holds true, thank you for joining me on this journey.

Within this book, you were provided with basic information for Kali Linux. As a reminder once more, Kali Linux is not a beginner's distro for Linux. If you have read this book and are entirely lost on several subjects, that is okay—but you may be better off starting with a beginner's book instead of one designed for people who know what they are doing and are interested in doing better and more.

Ultimately, your next step is entirely dependent upon you and what you think you want to do. Do you want to practice on the actual distribution of Kali Linux? You may go through the information and effort necessary to install your own copy that you can begin to use and discover.

If you feel like Kali Linux is not right for you, whether due to it being too difficult, too different, or simply because you do not know what you are doing, then you are probably better off with starting with something simpler, such as Ubuntu and Mint.

Yes, this point has been reiterated several times because it is that important. Even after having read through this guide, if you are not entirely confident in yourself and your abilities, it may be better for you to forego Kali Linux temporarily while you build up your skills—and that is okay.

Perhaps at this point, you have taken the advice of the final chapter in this book and have decided to look into Python as well, bettering your scripting abilities so you will be able to better utilize your own commands.

That is also a fantastic decision to make and will help guide you on your journey as well, simply because you will have that much more knowledge.

No matter what you choose to do next, whether it is pursuing more knowledge about Linux in general or attempting to figure out how best to interact with Kali Linux that you have already installed, one thing is for sure: You have hopefully learned something during the process of reading this book. It is with the utmost hope as this book wraps to a close that you have found this book informative, helpful, and insightful to the grand world of Kali Linux and everything it has to offer. No matter whether you are a newbie or someone with familiarity with other Linux distros, good luck on your endeavors, and remember—just because you feel like things may be complicated now does not mean that you have to give up on it. You can put in the effort to learn if you want to, and with that effort will come results. Good luck and remember to keep your penetration testing ethical.

Dear Reader

Thank you for choosing to read my book out of the thousands that merit reading.

If you enjoyed it, please visit the site where you purchased it and leave a brief review.

Your feedback is very important to me and it will be very helpful to other readers, helping them to decide whether to read the book too, thanks!

Printed in Great Britain
by Amazon